Citizenship, identity and belonging in Kenya

Citizenship, identity and belonging in Kenya

University of Nairobi & SAMOSA-Festival Colloquium

Edited by
Zarina Patel & Zahid Rajan

Daraja Press

Published by Daraja Press

http://darajapress.com

© Samosa Festival 2017

All rights reserved.

Cover design: Catherine McDonnell

Library and Archives Canada Cataloguing in Publication

University of Nairobi & SAMOSA-Festival Colloquium (2016 : Nairobi, Kenya)
Citizenship, identity and belonging in Kenya : University of Nairobi; SAMOSA-Festival Colloquium /
edited by Zarina Patel & Zahid Rajan.

Papers from the University of Nairobi Department of Literature and AwaaZ
SAMOSA Festival Joint Literary Colloquium held as part of the 2016
AwaaZ SAMOSA Festival held in Nairobi, Kenya, 9-27 July 2016.
Includes bibliographical references.
Issued in print and electronic formats.
ISBN 978-0-9953474-7-2 (softcover).–ISBN 978-0-9953474-8-9 (ebook)
1. Nationalism and the arts–Kenya–Congresses. 2. Arts–Kenya–Congresses.
3. Nationalism–Kenya–Congresses. 4. Kenyans–Race identity–Congresses. 5. Somalis–Race
identity–Kenya–Congresses. I. Patel, Zarina, 1935-, editor II. Rajan, Zahid, 1960-, editor III. SAMOSA
Festival (7th : 2016 : Nairobi, Kenya)
IV. Title.

NX180.N38C58 2017   700′.452996762   C2017-902343-8

C2017-902344-6

Contents

Introduction   1
Zarina Patel and Zahid Rajan

1. Constitution as a source of identity   3
   Keynote Address
   Yash Pal Ghai

2. Where are we now? The politics of becoming a Kenyan   7
   Sarah Nkuchia

3. Marked identities and diasporic belonging in M G   13
   Vassanji's 'The In-Between World of Vikram Lall'
   Jairus Omuteche

4. Identity and nationalism in M G Vassanji's 'The   25
   In-Between World of Vikram Lall'
   Orao James

5. The question of identity, dying and death: An analysis of   35
   Margaret Ogola's 'Place Of Destiny'
   Judith Jefwa

6. Identity and homecoming in 'The Kitchen Toto' and   45
   'Nairobi Half Life': Confronting the colonial and post
   colonial Kenya through the film
   Lencer Achieng' Ndede

7. Writing for the Kenyan stage from the year 2000: A   57
   practitioner's perspective
   John Sibi-Okumu

8. Kenyan-hood, identity and being: Tracing Kenya's   63
   identity and belonging in manner of speech and music
   forms
   Kanyi Thiong'o

9. Identity and musical score in Tosh Gitonga's 'Nairobi   75
   Half Life'
   Simon Peter Otieno

10. The forgotten citizens: A search for identity and   85
    belonging for women religious
    Jane Nambiri Ouma

11. The journey to identity, belonging and citizenship of the   97
     girl child in the traditional African home
     Joseph Muleka

12. Some reflections on the endurance of the human spirit in   109
     a refugee story
     Carey Baraka and Tom Odhiambo

13. Journey out of the state of statelessness: Kenya's   115
     unfinished business
     Wandia Njoya

14. Exile and identity: Representations of trauma in Warsan   125
     Shire's refugee poems: Souvenir and Home
     Lynda A Ouma

15. The wedding   131
     Ciarunji Chesaina

     About the contributors   141

     About the editors   147

     Acknowledgements   149

Introduction

Zarina Patel and Zahid Rajan

To understand the genesis of this colloquium we need to go back to 2004 – for that is the year that the first issue of *AwaaZ* magazine was published. 'AwaaZ' is an Indian word meaning 'Voices' and the magazine sought initially to 'voice' the history of South Asian leaders who had participated in Kenya's anti-colonial struggle. After some years the magazine moved on to address minority and diversity issues in Kenya and in the region. Today, it has to date 47 issues in its stable.

The central objective of the *AwaaZ* editors (Zahid Rajan and Zarina Patel) has been, and still is, the building of national unity in Kenya through mutual understanding, learning and interaction. In 2005, to achieve the latter, a festival was organised in Nairobi bringing together various communities in a celebration of art, music, dance, film and debate. The festival was called 'SAMOSA' which was both an acronym (South Asian Mosaic of Society and the Arts) as well as a popular Kenyan food which contains a variety of tasty mixes.

The 7th SAMOSA Festival, staged in July 2016, was held in the Eastleigh, Kamukunji constituency of Nairobi. This is one of the earliest settlements in the development of Nairobi originally largely South Asian but now home to diverse communities but with a preponderance of Kenyan Somalis and refugees from Somalia. SAMOSA is a grassroots festival that works with communities. By holding the festival in Eastleigh, the festival tried to dispel certain stereotypes which claim that:

- Somalis in particular, and the people of Eastleigh in general, are thieves, drug addicts and corrupt

- Somalis are 'terrorists'

- Eastleigh is an area of the 'Underworld' where dealing in stolen goods is the norm

In short, we wanted to dispel the myth that Eastleigh is a dangerous, no-go zone. Nothing is further from the truth. We moved about freely and met a people full of kindness, warmth, enterprise and thrift. But they are also a people deeply traumatized by the brutality of the Kenyan security forces.

A major concern for this Somali population is the issue of 'citizenship' and their ability and right to procure, as legitimate citizens of Kenya, national identity cards. It was to address these particular concerns that, as part of the SAMOSA festival, a colloquium was organized in collaboration with the

Literature Department of the University of Nairobi under the heading of 'Citizenship, Identity and Belonging'.

Fourteen papers were presented, the contributors drawn from various Kenyan universities, as well as two authors from civil society. While the issues of 'refugees', 'statelessness' and 'Kenyan-ness' were directly addressed, some unexpected essays stressed the relevance of the colloquium topic to 'Death and Dying', 'Women Religious' and to 'Speech and Music Forms'. The keynote address was given by Prof Yash Pal Ghai, the architect of Kenya's second constitution. He focused on the sections of the constitution which deal with the issues of citizenship, identity and belonging that were designed to ensure justice equality. It was a revealing reminder of the far-sighted, inclusive and just objectives of the 2010 Constitution.

In the period leading up to the next SAMOSA Festival (it is a biannual event), the SAMOSA team plans to organize various events and projects under the banner of 'mini-SAMOSAS'. We are planning a memorial lecture for Makhan Singh, the founder of Kenya's trade union movement. Given the growing labour unrest in Kenya and the on-going strikes by doctors and university lecturers, the subject is timely. In the pipeline too is a concert with the Indian flute and tabla as its central focus, as well as a multi-racial chess tournament. These endeavors will feed into the 8th SAMOSA to be held in 2018.

1.

Constitution as a source of identity

Keynote Address

Yash Pal Ghai

The *Samosa* Festival, organised for some years by Zahid Rajan and Zarina Patel, brings together a large number of communities and individuals, including distinguished academics—as is the case today. The activities this year have been particularly interesting and productive, involving as they have done a number of 'marginalised' communities, including the Somali residents of Eastleigh and their social and political leaders. There is no other avenue I know of where the arts and culture of Kenya's communities are celebrated and discussed by such mixed audiences.

The theme of this final session is *Identity*. It is dominated by Kenya's leading scholars of literature and arts. I have chosen to speak on the 2010 Constitution as a source of identity— national, communal and individual. In a world of literary scholars, I offer a few reflections on our new constitution—which I immodestly call the identity of the country and hopefully of its people. The concept of a constitution as identity is relatively new. In the old days the constitution was about the structure of the power of the state. Today we realise the complexity of the state and of its people. As I read some of the wonderful and scholarly papers that are on offer, I am struck about how frequently the authors are concerned to understand the identity of the people, group or community—and even sex—I should not say 'even sex'–but 'also sex'.

A major difference between the scholarly and the lawyers' approaches that strikes me is that the scholar studies identity as it defines a community or group, while a lawyer's major interest is often the shaping of identity—of the nation and the people. The constitution then becomes the primary instrument of shaping identity. Some commentators, including our immediately past Chief Justice, call such a constitution a 'transformative constitution'. This is an apt description of our present constitution.

I also notice in the scholarly work on offer the concern about the status or acceptance of a community, particularly in the papers about the Somali and other minorities—and there I felt that a constitutional lawyer and a literary scholar have found common ground. Kenya's constitution is about identity in a number of ways. First and foremost, it is about defining our identity as a people. This is stated upfront—in the preamble-where, in the name of the people, the constitution says that we are 'Proud of our ethnic, cultural and religious diversity, and determined to live in peace and unity as one indivisible sovereign nation'. It commits us to 'nurturing and protecting the wellbeing of individual, the family, communities and the nation'. It goes on to recognise 'the aspirations of all Kenyans for a government based on the essential values of human rights, equality, freedom, democracy, social justice and the rule of law'. The constitution, it reminds us, is a result of 'our sovereign and inalienable right to determine the form of governance of our country'—which indeed they have exercised in the making of the constitution.

Last week, our distinguished politician, or not so distinguished, Moses Wetang'ula chastised Raila Odinga, also a distinguished, or not so distinguished, politician. He was complaining that Raila was not sticking to his own tribe (or community as he delicately called it), but instead poking into the affairs of Wetang'ula's tribe— poking meaning trying to get their votes. He went on to say that Raila should leave the Luhya to Wetang'ula and his new found friends, just as he leaves the Kikuyu to Uhuru and the Kalenjin to Ruto—and presumably the Northeast to the Somalis, and the coast to the Arabs. Raila, he told us, can spend as much time as he likes with the Luo. Wetang'ula did not, I noticed, allocate any territory or community to the wahindi, leaving the likes of me without an identity. The trouble with Wetang'ula and other politicians is that they do not understand the Kenyan identity established in the constitution; or more likely do not care about it.

Transformative the constitution may be, but achieving transformation is no easy task. The constitution makes a valiant effort to bring about the right balance between diversity and nationhood. It is as much about values as it is about institutions—in fact institutions must take their cue from the values. Article 4 declares Kenya a multi-party democratic State founded on the national values and principles of government referred to in Article 10. These values bind all state institutions and people when performing state functions. Every Kenyan should know, but few do, what these values are. They include patriotism, national unity, democracy, human dignity, inclusiveness and equality, protection of the marginalised, participation, integrity and accountability. Many detailed provisions protect the languages, cultures, life styles and religions of Kenya's communities—thus recognising our diversity.

But for our present purposes, the more immediate issue is national unity or nationhood. The key to this is the political system. A key element is equal rights of all citizens—and if the government has not yet realised, that covers Somalis, Ogieks, Nubians, and coastal communities—and also that entitlement to an ID is an essential aspect of equal citizenship. Equally important is the nature of the broader political system. This is spelt out in the rules of the electoral system which are routinely violated by political parties—and which the IEBC either is not willing or not able to stop, especially secrecy, corruption, lack of transparency, violence, intimidation, and improper influence. The basic principles for nationhood pertain to the structure and principles of political parties—central to every democratic system. The constitution requires that every political party shall have a national character as set out in law, a democratically elected governing body, promote and uphold national unity, abide by the democratic principles of good governance, promote and practise democracy through regular, fair and free elections within the party, respect the rights of all persons to participate in the political process, including minorities and marginalised groups, and respect human rights including gender equality and equity.

And now we come to the sphere where diversity and nationhood are balanced. The constitution stipulates that a political party shall not be founded on a religious, linguistic, racial, ethnic, gender or regional basis or seek to engage in advocacy of hatred on any such basis. How many of our political parties have subscribed to the above principles? To defend an obvious crook because he is 'one of us' or make intertribal political deals, or hire goons to break up meetings of other political parties—all routinely done by political parties —is no way to build national unity.

This colloquium therefore is making an important contribution to ensuring that our national discourse is constantly reminded of the need for tolerance and understanding as we strive to build a united Kenya. I wish you all stimulating and fruitful deliberations.

2.

Where are we now? The politics of becoming a Kenyan

Sarah Nkuchia

Has anyone else noticed an odd experience that occurs when asked – 'are you Kenyan?' Even when the immediate and obvious response is 'yes', – depending on the particular time and space – the affirmative answer is sometimes accompanied by a nagging feeling of being trapped in an intricate web of complexity and tension. It feels like there is need to point out that the sense of belonging to Kenya is not always obvious neither is it always desirable. Sometimes, one would much rather say 'yes – but it's complicated.....' Kimani Njogu (2010) refers to a similarly complex reaction when Kenyans in the diaspora engaged in online chatrooms around the time of the 2007 elections. They observe that Kenyans abroad were frustrated by the instant assumptions made about them when their nationality or ethnicity was revealed.

Respectfully appreciating the multiple valid perspectives on the topic, the focus of this paper will be to partly unpack the writer's personal feelings of complexity and tension associated with the question of the Kenyan identity. It will attempt to face some of the nuanced details of being Kenyan, from my perspective as a young Kenyan woman and reflection on a few scholars' insights on national identity.

In discussing citizenship and identity, we often fall back to assumptions on the evolution of the state. There is a tendency to presume that states are formed through a neat historical sequence; gradually moving from nation building to the creation of a state. In other words, national identity and belonging is the foundation for citizenship. However, Anthony Smith (1986) points out that in practice, nations differ widely in substance and formation. There are ethnic based and territorial based nations. Some states evolve from nations which are ethnic based; relying on ties such as shared geology, history, culture and religion. These states are formed through years and years of national mobilization and politicization. On the other hand, there are also territorial based nations. These completely reverse the sequence, and are actually creations of the state; confined within the state's defined geographic boundaries and characterized by a political community, and a legal framework.

For certain, states formed after independence in Africa and elsewhere did not have the option of gradual evolution from ethnic nations to states. African states had to build nations on the basis of pre-defined territories. The major challenge though, was that states in Africa were also ethnically heterogeneous, and these diverse ethnic identities existed well before the state. Were these multiple ethnic identities to be an integral part of the formation of the nation, or were they to be overridden by a homogenized nationalist narrative? History confirms that the African nationalists chose the latter route, where ingrained in the nation-building project was an assumption that by allowing the state to overtly recognize ethnicity, the rifts within the population would be deepened which may lead to divided loyalties or secession. There was the general wish that ethnic identity would be washed away by the wave of nationalism.

With the benefit of hindsight, we now clearly see where this colossal assumption led us to. As Ilan Peleg (2004) points out, a non-inclusive process of nation building tends to 'ethnicize' the political entity, whereby the dominant ethnic group infuses their culture into that of the state to become what he refers to as the 'core nation'. In cases where the state is multi-ethnic, the domination of one or a few groups causes the isolation of other ethnic groups from the nation building project and its benefits, thereby causing or deepening ethnic divides and conflict. It produces a systemic and unquestionable ethnic hierarchical order which is internalized by the core nation and the other 'subordinate' ethnic groups.

From Wekesa's (2010) chapter 'Negotiating Kenyanness', we see how this process unfolded in Kenya. First, we are reminded that Kenya only existed as a fixed entity with a defined territory after the British named it a protectorate. It therefore became a territory long before it was conceived to be a nation. Kenya was inhabited by multiple communities for centuries before and during colonialism (Wekesa, 2010). These different ethnolinguistic communities came in different waves of migration, and interacted with each other through trade, cultural exchange but also through conflict. Though this interaction, they became interdependent on each other for survival. After a shared colonial struggle, rather than acknowledge that the formation of the nation would be legitimized through an appreciation of the collective struggle and cultural diversity, the focus shifted to conflate groups into a homogenized national identity (Wekesa, 2010).

To build this tenuous concept of the Kenyan nation, the state invested in the construction of a nationalist ideology. This ideology, infused with politics of power had to create and sustain a collective memory on which to build a nation. However, this state-imposed collective memory differed quite substantively from the memories that arose out of different communities within Kenya. The salient similarities and differences between the multiple memories of Kenya's past, particularly those of marginalized communities, were not adequately considered in the nation building project. Instead, Kenya saw a privileging of particular ethnic groups over others in the nation-building project, which ended up excluding and wounding almost every other ethnic group in the process, and creating a toxic ethnic order.

Therefore, there never really was a foundational social contract between the different races and ethnic groups with the state of Kenya. There was no genuine agreement on shared values based on respect and inclusivity that would bind Kenyans. Contrary to the assumption that an overarching nationalism would 'kill the tribe', ethnicity seeped in and inadvertently became one, if not the most, prominent political instruments for mobilization of political power and resources within the state, deeply compromising the nationalist project. Instead of becoming less ethnicized, the ethnic order crystalized in our collective psyche.

State-sanctioned memories continue to gloss over the different experiences of Kenyans sometimes violently silencing or erasing them as was seen most poignantly through the mishandling and shelving of the Truth, Justice and Reconciliation (TJRC) report. The Kenyan identity is therefore fused with resentment or apathy by the majority of Kenyans who live a lifetime of fundamental disagreement with the ethnic order Kenya is built on and the wounds that this order inflicts.

This has resulted in recurrent violence and stunted development. For certain, it demonstrates that nations cannot sustainably be built by conflating multi-ethnic societies into uni- or bi-ethnic social, economic and political order while the majority of the population is excluded.

The Kenyan state has never substantively analyzed or admitted the extent of the reality of the ethnic order that the ethnicized nation building project created. Consequently, we have spent the past 50 years, beating around the policy bushes, debating cyclical questions about our national identity: who is a Kenyan? What makes one a true Kenyan? These questions seem to pop up in the socio-political scene at different times; for different reasons and for different groups of people, but often, the responses are quite superficial. For example, Wekesa (2010) retrieves hazy memories of events in 2004 whereby several attempts were made to foreground the quest for the Kenyan identity. The two events were led by the then government spokesman, Alfred Mutua where the government urged Kenyans to reflect on and highlight Kenyans' collective achievements through the 'Week of National Focus' in December 2004 under the slogan of 'Najivunia kuwa Mkenya'. Before that, Wekesa (2010) reminds us that we also came up with a national dress in mid-2004. As a young girl about to go through a national ritual of form four exams at the time, I watched as the public engaged in critique and protest around those two events. To me, the protests introduced a sense of identity chaos and confusion. Why were we still discussing what it means to be Kenyan, 40 years after independence? Didn't the Rainbow Coalition just solve all our ethnic problems of division? Wasn't Moi the issue, so that now that he had gone we were all good? It was puzzling that these issues were still on the table. We were later to learn from the anti-corruption whistle-blower John Githongo that around the same time in 2004, Kenya was also undergoing one of the most significant corruption scandals – Anglo Leasing. What became of the dress, and week of national focus, which was to be an annual event, can only be speculated upon as the post-election violence of 2007/08 painfully reminded us just three years later that beneath the superficial slogans of 'TwajuvinuakuwaWakenya' divisions and corruption ran deep.

Since the post-election 2007/08, Kenyans have struggled to heal and put back the pieces of the ideal of 'Kenyanness'. This struggle to reclaim the nation and dismantle the ethnic order was pursued in various ways: a stab at transitional justice methods through the Truth, Justice and Reconciliation Commission (TJRC) and a couple of years later, the promulgation and implementation of the new constitution – which was to herald a new dawn for the nation building project. The new constitution gave Kenyans a basis for a new social contract with the state with shared values and a common cause (Ghai & Ghai, 2011). Through devolution, there would be an attempt to remedy the ethnic and regional injustices using decentralization of power and resources to counties.

In spite of all the effort and good intentions at the macro level to rework Kenya, the deeply ingrained notion of ethnic order cannot be solved by the constitution alone. It seems that year after year, whenever the questions of Kenyaness arise, they are still fraught with contestations at the public and interpersonal level – sometimes they are loud and sometimes the contestations are experienced in silence. Some contestations are enduring, for instance in Northern Kenya, the Coast and the question of belonging of Kenyan Asians and some are emerging – for instance the sense of new marginalization emanating from the county structures.

Let me illustrate how, on an intrapersonal level, the interaction of Kenyans has changed very little on a psycho-sociological level in spite of the constitution:

Kenyans relish in the ability to meet someone, do a quick head to toe analysis, ask for the person's two names and instantaneously pigeonhole that person within the set ethnic order. As Njogu (2010) correctly points out, Kenyans and even non-Kenyans, are quick to place an ethnic label on a person from and decide their most probable cultural, political and social affiliations based on the most dominant narratives at the time. This instant labeling often creates dilemmas and heightens anxieties around the complexity of the Kenyan identity. In extreme cases, such as the 2007/8 post-election, such profiling costed far too many people their lives, limbs and property. For those of us that cannot and will not be neatly fixed within the ethnic order, this is frightening. Here is a personal example: my family has lived in Loitokitok for four generations now. Under the new constitutional dispensation, it is difficult to understand why I have to explain myself more, not less – that though my family is not all Maasai, Loitokitok is my home and Kajiado is my county. As I am made up of several communities, I am unable to fit neatly within the lines of all of them. Therefore, with a deep respect I prefer not to be strongly associated with the ethnic order, but rather to be identified as collection of all my different heritages.

Even though I speak Kiswahili fluently – the sole national language – and want to believe the hashtag #WeAreOne, it often goes unrecognized that there are those of us, that look and sound like we should have no problem belonging to Kenya, and yet we do. This is deeply ironic. You would have thought that as a result of generations of intermarriage, the children of multiple ethnic groups would be deemed a form of our national progression towards greater unity. You would have thought that this fusion of cultures and bringing together of families is something we would be proud of a as a country as a demonstration of our interconnectedness.

However, in the actual sense, the post-election violence deeply betrayed those of us who are a lose collective of ethnic communities and made us fear for our lives in this entho-centric country. It is clear to me that Kenya will give me its passport, but will never allow me to fully belong until I get behind an ethnic group, learn their language and vote according to the ethnic order. In socio-political practice, Kenya is deeply disrespectful of the decision to claim multiple heritages and the fluidity of our identity. But it is often much, much worse than my experience. Kenya can also be brutal to those who do not fit in the ethnic order. I empathize with the Kenyans of Asian heritage, and Kenyans of Somali heritage who, generation after generation are often never even given a chance to explain their Kenyanness but are met with violence and exclusion for not fitting in the ethnic order.

Ultimately though, I feel sorry for all Kenyans, because if you look closely, at the apex of the ethnic order, you will find that it is not an ethnic community that sits on top. But rather a group of self-serving politicians from different ethnic groups united by a predatory and rabid capitalist ideology and sanctioned by the neoliberal order that continues to colonize Africa.

Because of these painful complexities, supra-identities such as East African or Pan-African have become a fort of refuge to define, regroup and strategize in the struggle to emancipate ourselves from mental slavery, neocolonialism and the trappings of false ethnic hierarchies. It is my hope that as East African integration forges forward, the 'sting of ethnic animosity' and exaggerated emphasis on ethnicity for power and resources will be minimized in the long run. But even as I situate myself in these supra-identities, I am occasionally reminded that I should not give up on redefining the Kenyan identity altogether.

Just a band, my favorite Kenyan band, gives me hope. It is a band that cannot neatly be confined within what we assume is 'Kenyan' and yet they are Kenyan. They, a collective of ultra-creative young men from different ethnic groups who decided to make music using digital technology. To me, they represent a possibility of what we can become. Theirs is a futuristic and inspiring sound that moves us forward in our imagination, beyond the boundaries of what Kenyan youth 'should be' to what they 'can be'. They have offered leadership, in the construction of a non-ethnic based community of young Kenyans.

May we all find something that allows us to create a new national identity outside of the ethnic order. Kenya ni Kwetu.

Works Cited

Ghai, Y P, & J C 2011. *Kenya's Constitution: An instrument for change.* Nairobi: Katiba Institute.

Njogu, K, Ngeta, K, &Wanjau, M (2010). *Ethnic diversity in Eastern Africa.* Nairobi: Twaweza Communications.

Peleg, I (2004). Transforming ethnic orders to pluralistic regimes: Theoretical, comparative and historical analysis. In *Democracy and ethnic conflict: Advancing peace in deeply divided societies.* New York: Palgrave Macmillan. 7-26

Smith, A D (1988). *The ethnic origins of nations.* Oxford: Blackwell.

Wekesa, P W (2010). Negotiating Kenyanness, the debates. In M W Mungai & G Gona (Eds.), *(RE)membering Kenya* Vol. 1, 50-70). Nairobi: Twaweza Communications.

3.

Marked identities and diasporic belonging in M G Vassanji's 'The In-Between World of Vikram Lall'

Jairus Omuteche

Abstract

From historical accounts, human existence on earth has by nature been characterised by movement across geographical spaces-places. Some movements have been marked by permanent removal from one space-place to another, while others are marked by temporary immigration. In both cases there are varied motivations for an individual or groups to move from one geographical area to another. The contemporaneous phenomenon which has been termed as 'globalisation' cannot be understood outside the age old wheeling of populations around the globe. This reached a peak at the height of European imperialism from the 16th century to early 20th century spurred by heightened industrialisation and efficient communication. This period saw the expansion of military and economic – hence social, cultural and political – dominance over the world by Europe. Though this modern imperialism replicated the historical trends in empire conquest, expansion and occupation; it surpassed the Greek, Roman, Turkish, Islamic, and other such imperial expansions. The nature of colonial subject-hood and diasporic identities and belonging that M G Vassanji represents in his novel, 'The In-Between World of Vikram Lall', are informed by the impacts of the planetary movements and displacements that were a direct result of this European imperialism. These are identities that are negotiated in social environments characterised by cultural differences and diversities, power hierarchies, and global economic inequalities. The paper proposes to assess these variegated realities that are depicted in the story of the Lall family.

14

Key words: Globalisation, Imperialism, Identities, Belonging, Diaspora.

The Interface between Globalisation and Diaspora

Diasporas as products of movements reveal the transformative effects of journeys. These journeys, undertaken within globalized world phenomena, result in diasporic space-places which exert pressure and trigger evolution of new identities for both the host societies and the immigrants in the long term. In the ensuing interaction, the in-group and the outer-group are bound to re-adjust and some aspects of dialogue accrue. The writer constructs these experiences by situating experiences of the characters depicted in cross-currents of movement, border-crossings, and transnational interactions. The drama that their life experiences depicted is enacted on the backdrop of expanding globalization, 'state-of-the-art technology, frenzied capital mobility and neo-liberal policies'. Nevertheless these globalization flows are characterized by neo-imperial discriminations and inequalities perpetuated through exclusionary and containment strategies against large segments of world populations outside the core centres of global wealth concentrations.

The word 'diaspora' in its original meaning and in most of its usage suggests dispersed or exiled people, or forcibly deported populations whose removal may have included genocide, who are away from 'home' or their origin. Hence, there is usually a sense of 'homelessness', 'painful memories', or 'wish to return' that connect a diasporic people or community and links them in common memory to the lost-original 'home' they have been forced from (Tatla 1999, and Cohen 1999).

Diaspora communities are also usually under different pressures as they struggle to settle as minorities, adding aspects of re-negotiation and struggle for survival and acceptance to the understanding of the concept 'diaspora'. This understanding of diaspora can account, in a way, for the diasporic identities depicted in Vassanji due to some aspects of apparent compulsion in the original immigration of Asians into East Africa, though not of the same intensity and scale of victimhood reminiscent of classical Jewish diaspora or African American ones.

How is home and identity experienced in the diaspora within the reality of displacement and globalisation? Physicality of movement from one space-place to the other informs the interface between globalisation and diaspora. Some movements are forced while others are not, but still the seemingly self-willed movements may have some element of coercion. The push factors are what forces one to leave the original home, pull factors are the anticipated or enticing factors in the receiving community. Push factors may be characterised by pressure placed on the individual or group psychologically or economically.

When one speaks of diaspora one is talking of displaced groups moving across borders, leaving behind what they originally consider ancestral homelands. As Braziel and Mannur note, "Diaspora can perhaps be seen as a naming of the other which has historically referred to displaced communities of people who have been dislocated from their native homeland through the movements of migration, immigration, or exile" (2003: 1).

Lechner says that globalisation implies "the growth of ties that span space", leading more people becoming "connected across larger distances in different ways [...] creating a new world society in which they do more similar things, affect each other's lives more deeply, follow more of the same norms, and grow more aware of what they share"(2009: 1). Marked by intertwining processes with inherent diversity and inequalities, globalisation is multi-dimensional and multi-directional, creating "a new framework for social life around the globe" (Lechner, 2009: 1-2).

For Russell and Teitelbaum, discussions of international migration "must deal simultaneously at the levels of global trends, national, community and household conditions, and individual behaviours" (1992: 5). Therefore they see a link between migration and globalisation, which must inform the theorisation of diasporas.

As ongoing processes, globalisation, immigration, and resulting diasporas are constantly re-inscribed as groups and individuals continuously re-work and re-negotiate their identities. Choice and constraint permeate the dynamics of migration and the migrant and host communities' relationships to 'home'. Van Hear recognises this when he notes that the examination of force and choice in the shaping of diasporic identities must encompass the analysis of the migrant and the host communities and those who remain in the sending community (1998: 54). This awareness in the research will help us understand the processes of diasporic integration and socio-cultural or symbolic relationships of the immigrants to their natal home depicted in selected works. Within these contexts, the migrants re-construct diasporic home in *The In Between World*.

As diaspora essentially imply cumulative immigration and longevity of settlement, questions such as raised by Rosello arise, "[d]oes 'integration' mean that the stranger, after accepting a nation's hospitality, can finally offer hospitality, that is, not reciprocate, but lengthen the chain of possibly incommensurable hospitable gestures?" (2001: 18). Such considerations displace any aspects or perspectives that privilege fixity or clear linearity in appreciating the development of diasporic belonging and identity.

The making of the colonial subject-hood: The evolution of transformative and marked identities

From colonial times, Kenya's identity has been marked by transformation and marked-ness. This has been a result of the nature of cultural and power relations came to define the colonial society. For the colonized, their identities developed in conditions of political, economic and social state of dependency. According to W H New, creative and material production and sets of attitudes in dependent communities in practice "reflect the norms of the controlling culture" (1996: 102). In colonial situations, there exist varied levels of power discrepancies – gender, racial, class, economic and political centre and their marginalised peripheries. In the situation of Kenya which was colonised by Britain, the British were situated as the ideal norm. Through spectacles of power of power display, material consumption, cultural overwriting through education and religion, the colonized were trained to look at the British as the superior group. These processes also "trained the colonised to accept their connection with the empire as their only access of greatness" (New, 1996: 103) even though they were in all circumstances reduced to positions of social negligibility. New goes to posit that the main strategy of ensuring European supremacy in racial hierarchies in the colonised places "lay in the way the trappings of authority made imperial judgements seem the norm of civilized behaviour" (1996: 107). Vassanji depicts numerous instances of British colonial interpellation of their sense of power and racial superiority in colonial Kenya. An illustrative example is the description of the racial, power, and gender undertones of a cricket match between the Europeans in the Nakuru Club:

> Across from this eatery was a long and high grey wall, beyond which was the posh, exclusive Nakuru Club. Non-whites were not permitted in the club, but on special occasions such as this one, an area of the pavilion was set aside for the Asians. The Europeans, dressed smartly in white, the ladies wearing hats, sat in the wide, open, raised veranda of the clubhouse or outside on the grass where tables had been laid out. African waiters moved about wearing long, white kanzus, green sashes across their fronts, and green fezzes (2003: 74).

In this excerpt numerous discourses of colonial identities and how they are worked and reinforced can be read. The demarcation and racialization of space is evident. Groups are segregated with European-only areas being endowed with higher power and economic investment hence status. Spectacles of mannerism reinforce the hierarchies, as evident in the dressing codes of European men, women and African workers. The dressing is a social and cultural code of ones place and power position. Even the seating arrangements and eating habits are racially and power choreographed displays. As New argues, "architecture and fashion, for example – in the design of triumphal arches, ladies dresses, and military uniforms – asserted power visually" (1996: 107).

The club as a microcosm of the colonial space too reflect the maintenance and display of long developed stereotypes that assign social status and value and that enhance British colonial masculine-power domination. Indeed, racism and patriarchy were twin-pillars in the construction of colonial social identities. As evident in the description in the excerpt, and literally in whole segments of the novel set in the colonial period, the black female is virtually absent from the colonised social space. The white males govern the institutions that ran the colony – the church, the army, the judiciary, the legislature, the public administration and the economic machinery. The white female is a symbol of delicacy and carrier of European moral purity and probity. She is the direct opposite of the black female who must never be seen due to her embodiment of the historical stereotype of the black female moral corruption (see Omuteche, 2013; Wood, 2002, and Pieterse, 1992). The black male is the lowest in the colonially operative racist hierarchy. The black male maintains the gentry-like life of luxury of the colonialist through slave-like labour. The Asians hold the ambiguous social position of the racial buffer zone. This is evident in the once-a-year admission into the club. For the coloniser, the 'other' is always placed into commoditised objects to serve the needs of the imperial centre and maintain the European's mindset of superiority.

Thus the Indian diaspora in Kenya first took root in a colonial situation. This diaspora was constructed at the delicate interface of negation and assertion. The negotiation of located-ness on local space and interconnection across the global space came to underpin its strategies of negotiating identities and belonging. Colonial policies of land, settlement, citizenship, racial hierarchies, and the way the Asian immigrants responded to these as they reworked their identity and belonging all have left a mark on how the diaspora has shaped. Consequently, diaspora life was full of tensions, contradictions and conflicts for the immigrants as they tried to form social membership in the new space-places. Such tensions and contradictions are evident in the life of Vikram in *The In-Between World*.

The people who make up the Nakuru milieu in which Vikram grows, which is transnational in nature, experience differing extends of intensity of displacements. What stands out is a persistent sense of uproot-ment and group tensions occasioned by the colonial racial segregation practice that alienate different racial groups in the town. Racial segregation and class differentiation lead to a situation where individuals and groups have to work out their identity and belonging by positioning the 'self' against the 'other'. It is this innate feature of identity formation in a society defined by hierarchised privileges that result in some individuals or groups experiencing marginalisation. Consequently, though the new community that colonialism has forged in Kenya is characterised by diversity and cultural multiplicity, the colonial racial constructions do not allow the emergent of a new transnational multicultural community.

Hence, colonial segregation catalyzed processes that can be understood in Salman Rushdie's words when he defines the contemporary reality of "hybridity, impurity, and intermingling" that leads to "transformation that comes of new and unexpected combinations of human beings, cultures, ideas, politics [...]" (1992: 394). These are identities that emerge from the variegated processes of intermingling and combinations in the context of a society defined by diverse cultural contacts, change, and transformation.

However, due to the power relations on the colonial space that privileged racial hierarchy rather than equality in diversity, the transformative multiculturalism that emerge are uneasy. Colonial identities were developed for the colonized people in conditions of political, economic, and social dependency. Thus the identities that emerge are marked by difference and otherness. As William New argues, the creative and material production and sets of attitudes about value, authority, and social priority in dependant communities "in practice reflect the norms of the controlling culture" (1996: 102).

Under the prevailing conditions, everyone has to try to re-forge new identity and belonging in the new pace-places that is colonial Kenya. Vassanji depicts the impact of intense sense of displacement felt by Vikram as he grows up as an Indian boy in colonial Kenya. He experiences a split sense of belonging. One day after playing with Njoroge, Vikram is acutely aware of his fractured sense of identity and belonging in the midst of a world defined by difference and diversity:

I do recall that his being different, in features, in status, was not far from my consciousness. I was also aware that he was more from Africa than I was. He was African, I was Asian. His black skin was matte, his woolly hair impossibly alien. I was smaller, with pointed elvish ears, my skin annoyingly 'medium', as I described it then, neither one (white) nor the other (black). (2003: 27).

Later on, in relation to Njoroge, the black, and Bill, the white, Vikram thinks, "In that fateful year of our friendship, when we played together I couldn't help feeling that both Bill and Njoroge were genuine, in their very different ways; only I, who stood in the middle, Vikram Lall, cherished son of an Indian grocer, sounded hollow like a bad penny" (*The In-Between World*, 54). But at the same time, the boy intensely wants to identify with his home, Kenya (2003: 121). He works out his identity and situates his belonging by embracing the Kenya space-place. This is evident in descriptive passages in the novel that reveal Vikram's and generally the Asian's strong affinity to the Kenyan landscape. This connection is especially articulated in the description of the relationships of the Asian communities to the railway line and the towns and business that sprouted along it. Vikram observes this when they travel for a holiday to Mombasa:

At every stop Indians got on or off, and there were people who were known to my family. For in each town was an Indian main street, with the same squat shop-houses of brick, with stores similar to those I was familiar with in Nakuru. (2003: 121).

It is during this journey that Vikram embraces the beauty of the land that is his adopted home, "But this, all around me, was mine, where I belong with my heart and soul" (2003: 121). This memory connects him to his ancestors, hence the history of the Indian immigrant in Kenya. Vikram Lall's grandfather, Anand Lall Peshawari came to Kenya alongside many others from his ancestral homeland of India who were brought in by the British colonial authorities to work on the Kenya Uganda railway (2003: 16). This was the first instance of translocation of East African Asians, which was part of the imperial reworking of people's geographies of belonging in the lands they invaded and colonised. The Lall family lives in Nakuru, but all over Kenya there are Asian Africans, who like Vikram's family, came as railway workers to Kenya in the 1890s.

Landscape and the negotiation of diasporic rooted-ness: The emergence of diasporic subject-hood and postcolonial challenges

The negotiation of identities and belonging, even when they are defined by global fluidity or hyphenation (Indian-Kenyan), seem to still coalesce around bounded space-places – house, neighbourhood, city/town/state, or country as nation state. Hence analysis of diaspora in a globalised world can reveal the complexity and paradoxes of localised identities and assertion of belonging of individuals and groups who find themselves in widespread global network and planetary inter-dependency.

While Appadurai enunciates well the global; Savage, Bagnall, and Longhurst likewise enunciate well the local. Appadurai identify global flows in terms of characteristic '-scapes' of globalisation which are interrelated but at the same time stand-alone irregular flows. These are ethnoscapes – the moving of individuals and communities such as tourists, immigrants, refugees, exiles, transnational communities, planetary travellers and others; technoscapes – flows of technology and information across boundaries; financescapes – flows involving currency markets, financial and currency investments and speculations; mediascapes – encompassing planetary dissemination and proliferation of media products, broadcasts and images; and ideoscapes – proliferation of political ideologies and diffusions of political ideas/concepts (1996: 33-37). Savage, Bagnall, and Longhurst on their part too identify five constructions of the local in the context of constructing identity and situating belonging: "There are in fact five ways of constructing the 'local' [...] first the local as context, secondly the local as the 'particular' in opposition to the global 'universal'; thirdly the local as historical residue, fourthly the local as hub in a network and fifthly the locality as bounded construction" (2005: 4).

These conceptions of the global and the local can help us understand the diasporic identities of Asians in Kenya that emerged after independence. For one, certain circumstances of history led arguably to the global expansion of the Asian diaspora. At the dawn of independence, many Kenyan Asians opted to immigrate to Britain. This is described as a mass exodus by Vikram:

A mass migration began, as thousands took to the planes almost overnight [...] The Nairobi sky reverberated with airplanes leaving at all hours [...] So many friends and acquaintances left; families were torn apart; stores which had been landmarks for decades vanished, personalities who had been fixtures in our social lives departed. (2003: 273).

This mass migration complicates the diasporic identities of Asians, making them decadently global and transnational. But the definition of the diaspora remain largely grounded and defined in terms of space-places hence landscape remains a key feature in reworking and re-negotiating the emerging identities and sense of belonging. Hence the local and the global intermingle.

The Asians who immigrated to Europe via Kenya return to the country where they have family ties and feel strong historical and cultural ties. For these Asians, Kenya has evolved into a secondary site of cultural belonging where they have strong historical, economical and cultural links, with Europe and America becoming the 'diasporas'. Thus Shobha Devi, an Asian British whose family immigrated to Britain by way of Kenya, come back 'home' to marry. She ends up Vikram's wife through the arrangement of their two families (2003: 307).

When the Lall family moves to Nairobi, just like in Nakuru, Vikram as an individual and their family as part of Asian community, appropriate the space-place in the adopted home and assert their belonging as they construct viable identity. What the process of asserting belonging and re-negotiating identity reveal is the nature of diasporic atmosphere they are worked in. There is the acute consciousness of 'other' and 'otherness' that entails a sense of de-centring of personhood in the migrants: Vikram always feels exposed, apart, and sometimes a victim of discrimination.

In Nairobi the post-independent sociocultural landscape is informed by tensions and contradictions. At independence, the community that emerge is characterised by racial, class, economic, political, and cultural diversity. Each group evolve distinct social membership and cultural identity. Vikram notes the apparent racial and social 'othering' that define the new town's landscape. Neighbourhoods, businesses, and social places are bounded, based on some type of sameness, excluding 'others'. Asians have their own estates and Africans theirs, which more than being racially defined, they are more and more becoming features of class stratification of the newly independent nation.

The schools Vikram and his sister Deepa attend are differentiated. They attend predominantly Asian only schools; racial segregation has evolved into class stratification. The available employment for the Asians in the economy is also exclusionary. Vikram feels that the Asian Africans are hemmed into certain social and economic roles. His experiences in the civil service, and the way he is finally forced out are illustrative.

This is the time the relationship between Njoroge and Deepa, Vikram's sister, deepens and acquires decidedly romantic overtones. The fragmented and marked identities that have entranced difference rather than multiculturalism among the different cultural groups make relating across groups difficult and even unacceptable by some groups. Vikram's parents cannot hear of Deepa marrying an African. The confrontation between the young generation and the old parents that ensue on this question of love and marriage across races dramatise how far marked identities came to define the newly independent nation. While Deepa loves and would marry Njoroge, the parents insist she marry an Asian like herself. Her father's reaction to her instance of independent choice of a love partner is illustrative:

> What do you mean you will marry anyone whom you want? Papa exploded. We are not Europeans, remember that, we are desis, Indians. Proud Indians, we have our customs, and we marry with the permission and blessings of our parents! You will do as you are told, girl! (2003: 201).

Vikram further notes that the marked-ness of differentiated identities are complex and deeply entrenched. So for him, his sister's unilateral secret acceptance of Njoroge's proposal without consulting her parents not only flaunted the family norms, but also the established norms of cultural separateness that were becoming entrenched:

> She did not seem to understand the seriousness of her offence, not to me but to the values of our times and people. We did not marry blacks or whites, or low-castes or Muslims; there were other restrictions, too subtle for us of the younger generation to follow; Hindu Punjabis were the strong preference always. (2003: 202).

It is this transgressive daring of Deepa that defines Vassanji's critique of the predominant variegated singularities in the Asian diaspora in East Africa. The regimentation of identities prevented the emergence of a truly multicultural society.

It is the same case for Vikram too, when he goes to study in Dar-es-salaam and meets Yasmin, a Shamsi Muslim girl. There is always between them an uneasy consciousness of the lines of difference that separate them culturally, historically, and socially. Vikram remembers that whenever he met Yasmin outside the college Shamsi mosque and walked together to the dinning room, they were followed by "a gauntlet of very pregnant stares" (2003: 211). This points to how differences, puritanical cultural loyalties, and social controls in in-groups that have been accentuated undermine the flourishing of the possible mutual multiculturalism.

Through Vikram's description of his experience with Yasmin in Dare-es-salaam, Vassanji censures this serious failure of multicultural diasporic identities in East Africa:

> I had been to her house on the way to some place else, once, and on another occasion for Sunday luncheon. I knew that her parents, although courteous and hospitable on the surface, were intensely against their daughter hitching up with me, a Hindu Punjabi; her two brothers were brief to the point of rudeness – because I was 'par-comm,' an outsider […] (2003: 211).

So Yasmin, like all females from Asian diasporic communities in East Africa depicted in the novel are heavily policed by their families lest they transgress culturally. The myth of group purity plays out leading to persistent contestation of each culture's space in the multiplicity. We have to read in this persistent contestation the fact of the nature and role of culture in a community's collective psychological survival. Each cultural group tends to emphasis its folk culture. This resilience of folk culture leads to marked-ness as the group seeks to re-define its sense of being in the diasporic space. Through the emphasis of original folk culture, the individuals and group are able to evolve psychological strategies that re-align the cultural transformation. At the end these cultural transformations are emergent and new as they are worked dialogically, and are realised as already marked.

Nevertheless, the Asians in Africa have managed to work out a new form of belonging and create some aspect of localism and communitarism in their new space-place in Kenya to deal with the challenges of diasporic assertion of home. As Vikram states "we have been Africans for three generations, not counting my own children", Kenya has become their home. They have reconstructed their belonging and established cultural and social institutions that tie them to the local landscape culturally and spiritually. Historically they have experienced and taken part in the colonial and postcolonial experiences the country has gone through. They have overcome prejudice, suspicion, and even blackmail (2003: 328-330, 342).

The generational level of the immigrants may influence how they relate to the host. While Vikram's mother was born in India and came to Kenya as a bride, his father was born in Kenya during the height of colonialism. The mother is the more stubborn in enforcing differentiated identifications for the family.

References

Appadurai, A 1996. *Modernity at Large: Cultural Dimensions of Globalisation* (Minneapolis: University of Minnesota Press).

Braziel, J E and Mannur, A 2003. 'Nation, Migration, Globalisation: Points of Contention in Diaspora Studies'. In Jana Evans Braziel and Anita Mannur (eds.) *Theorizing Diaspora: A Reader* (Oxford: Blackwell Publishing) pp. 1-22.

Cohen, R 1999. 'Rethinking "Babylon": Iconoclastic Conceptions of the Diasporic Experience.' In Steven Vertovec and Robin Cohen (eds.) *Migration, Diasporas and Transnationalism* (Cheltenham: Edward Elgar Publishing) pp. 252-279.

Hoogvelt, Ankie. 'Globalization and the Postcolonial World,' in David Held & Anthony McGrew (ed.) *The Global Transformations Reader: An Introduction to the Globalization Debate*, (Cambridge: Polity, 2000) pp. 355-60.

Lechner, F J 2009. *Globalization: The Making of World Society*. Oxford: Wiley-Blackwell.

New, W H (1996). 'Colonial Literatures.' In Bruce King (ed.) *New National and Post-Colonial Literatures: An Introduction*. (Oxford: Clarendon Press) pp. 102-119.

Omuteche, J 2013. 'Re-representation of home in Ngugi wa Thiong'o and Toni Morrison: (Re)Vision of Identity and Belonging.' Unpublished PhD Dissertation, University of Sunderland.

Pieterse, J N (1992). *White on black: Images of Africa and blacks in western popular culture*. New Heaven: Yale University Press.

Rosello, M 2001. *Postcolonial Hospitality: The Immigrant as a Guest* (California: Stanford University Press).

Rushdie, S (1992). *Imaginary Homelands*. Harmondsworth: Penguin.

Russell, S and Teitelbaum, M 1992. *International Migration and International Trade*. World Bank discussion Paper 160 (Washington DC: World Bank).

Savage, M, Bagnall, G, and Longhurst, B 2005. *Globalisation and Belonging* (London: Sage Publications).

Tatla, D S 1999. *The Sikh Diaspora: The Search for Statehood* (London: UCL Press).

Van Hear, N 1998. *New Diasporas: The Mass Exodus, Dispersal and Regrouping of Migrant Communities*. London: UCL Press.

Vassanji, M G (2003). *The In-Between World of Vikram Lall*. Edinburgh: Canongate.

Wood, M (2002). *Slavery, empathy, and pornography*. Oxford: Oxford University Press.

4.

Identity and nationalism in M G Vassanji's 'The In-Between World of Vikram Lall'

Orao James

Abstract

One must write for one's age, so says Sartre, arguing that the writer needs to go beyond a passive reflection of his/ her age to wanting to maintain it or change it (1988: 243). But there is really no such thing as a passive reflection where history is concerned and the need for constant questioning of held or handed down beliefs, as propagated by the postmodern approaches, re-situates the writer and his/her audience into newer and more dynamic definitions of and reflections on that age. This dynamism demands a continuous refinement, through constant negotiations, of what makes up the age of a writer and his/her history.

M G Vassanji in The In-Between World of Vikram Lall presents, through a kaleidoscopic constellation of characters, a way to look at Kenya's history around those defining moments of the struggle for independence and thereafter. It thus refocuses the question not only of history but also of identity – by weaving tales that encapsulate all prevalent discourses of what has made Kenya. Kenya's identity; its nationhood and the nationalist movements that informed that identity of a nation are re-cast and re-presented for dynamic discourses.

This paper seeks to discuss the notions of identity and especially how it is informed by nationalist movements. Vassanji, in all his books, has consistently attempted to situate the often ignored 'Afro-Asian' within the often ethnocentric African history. In this text, this attempt is placed within the backdrop of several histories and as such it reflects, not passively, but actively and questioningly and at certain points even subversively on what it means to be Kenyan; a question

26

that is also at the core of this paper. Not the least important in this paper is also the question of for which age Vassanji was writing.

Keywords: Identity, nationalism, history, African-Asian, Vassanji.

Literature as subversive history

'Novels arise out of the shortcomings of history', so said Novalis. And because of its ability to offer alternative takes on sanctioned myths and histories, a novel can and does challenge history, both the private and the public versions. And in so doing a novel can and does offer sites for questioning officialdom, for questioning the self and for questioning the family myths and in effect for questioning identities. M G Vassanji's novel unravels several myths of nationhood, recreates histories and questions the role of the African-Asians in the struggle for Kenya's independence and the aftermath of the nationalist movements. It describes the lives of an Asian family in Nakuru during the state of emergency years, moves to Nairobi during the post-independence euphoria and upheavals and back and forth weaving a constellation of relationships between the African-Asians and other 'Kenyans', providing a kaleidoscope of ties, friendships and betrayals that in the end paint the picture of Kenya as a nation.

But to ask with Rushdie (2010: 13), does literature seek to do more than describe, or can it open more doors? While not laying claim to historical accuracy, this novel, nevertheless, seeks to open more doors: it seeks to break a silence; to give voice to a people neglected in historical accounts of Kenya's nationalism and nationhood; to present a "plausible 'truth', while based on [not so] fictitious characters and events" (Black, 2000: 87). It at once gives voice to the children and grandchildren of those indentured Indians who built the railway, while at the same time challenging their sometime self-imposed non-belonging, with feet planted in both countries, ready to flee, when one place gets too hot (Vassanji, 2005: 342). In effect, it sets itself against the "truth-discourses" (Black, 2000: 87) of history and belonging by providing an *other* plausible history; effectively reigniting the discourse on Kenyan-ness. As Rushdie puts it, "[…] literature can, and perhaps must, give the lie to official facts." (Rushdie, 2010: 14). In a post-colonial setup this novel has effectively "been put in the position of telling truths that the official discourses of […] history cannot speak." (Black, 2000: 92) By so doing it brings to the fore the question of identity and belonging of the African-Asian in Kenya.

By taking a subversive stance against official historical discourses and by purporting to recount tales about the search for and construction of identities, the novel becomes political (questions of identity and belonging are inherently political); it posits questions that have been ignored in the officially propagated accounts by allowing voices hitherto silenced to come forth and muddy the neat accounts that make up official history. By allowing these voices, the novel thus offers a forum through which tales of belonging and identity of the few others can intermingle with the already sanctioned voices of the majority; if not to challenge these sanctioned voices, then to expand the repertoire of identities that make up the nationhood of Kenya.

Identity as an act of telling stories

Identity in this case is understood as a matter of telling stories, as Whitebrook also asserts:

> I suggest that identity is, primarily, a matter of stories persons tell others about themselves, plus stories others tell those persons and/or other stories in which those persons are included. [...] the construction of identity – narrating identity – entails placing the self in the public sphere [...]. (Whitebrook, 2001: 4)

And as Vikram Lall, the main character in this novel, says in the prologue, "[...] I simply crave to tell my story." (Vassanji, 2005: 1) This statement is a plea to be seen as a member of the nation Kenya. It summarizes the question of identity in the novel. Lall's story is, of course, as revealed in the many pages of the book, not just HIS story, but also THE History of a people, a country and a nation. His story weaves in and out, encapsulating the history, stories and myths of diverse peoples, with the end result that an identity of a nation emerges, only to be suspended, revised and retold.

Lall's story is his attempt to position himself, and in effect his people, in the narrative of Kenya's nationhood. He tries to affirm his *Kenyan*-ness:

> We have been Africans for three generations, not counting my own children. Family legend has it that one of the rails on the railway line just outside the Nakuru station has engraved upon it my paternal grandfather's name, Anand Lal Peshawari, in Punjabi script – and many another rail of the line has inscribed upon it the name and birthplace of an Indian labourer (p. 16).

This is Lall putting his family into the public sphere, scripting them into the nation-building narrative. India (where the public narrative tries to place him and his family) remains a "fantasyland", a place where "my father – proudly Kenyan, hopelessly [...] colonial – went to [...] once, and brought back my mother" (p. 21). The othering narrative placing them in India and as such as non-Kenyans is repudiated by one affirming their Kenyan identity: "I knew of no world outside my Nakuru, this home, this backyard, the shopping centre, the school; [...]" (p. 54).

And in a country struggling to find its nationhood, identity in whichever form it takes becomes foremost; its documentation is an act of invention and the cacophony of voices raised in contesting storytelling of the straggling nation drowns out the voices of the minority groups, who did not have a Jomo Kenyatta as a rallying figure-head. But Lall's story rewrites this part of the history too and identifies himself with Kenyatta the purported Mau Mau leader in the form of an oath Njoroge administers to him: "All those secrets I have told you, you will not tell them to anybody? [...] I will not tell anybody. [...] You must take an oath. I will take an oath" (p. 104). He further writes his uncle, Mahesh, into the Mau Mau narrative by crafting him as a collaborator, who went out of his way, risking his relationships with his immediate family to supply provisions, medication and even a pistol to the outlawed fighters.

Lall's story also exposes a weakness in the construction of identity through narration. The official storytellers of the budding nation forgot a very important aspect of identity: the identity of a dynamic entity, as the budding nation was then, could only be fluid. This fluidity is shown in the novel as the narration transitions from Mau Mau uprisings to the post-independence period. Those that thought they belonged find themselves questioning their own belonging and in effect the nationhood, the identity, of the newly independent state. Njoroge, who had impressed upon Lall the messianic character of Kenyatta (p. 53), later turns around and warns him to use a long spoon while dining with the devil. While during the emergency it was the privileged classes, the Europeans and the Asians, who called Kenyatta *daitya*, in the post-independent Kenya it is the former devotee Njoroge who sees in him the Devil. Not only is Lall's story and its accuracy, or maybe his interpretation of events, put into disrepute, the whole narrative of the nationalist movement is also in effect questioned. The incompleteness and shakiness of the narrated myth of nationalism demand new stories.

But it is not only the nationhood that is portrayed as in flux. The very identity as Africans and Kenyans that Lall tries to narrate for himself and his people keeps changing; sometimes as self-positioning, sometimes as an act of othering by entitled Kenyans. As Lall himself says, especially of his parents' generation: "For now [...] they were too inconsistent and confused about where they stood and who they were, even as they called themselves Kenyans" (p. 173). The state of flux seems to increase with the relaxing of the once inviolable distinctions along class and prestige lines. While during the emergency period Lall and his family gladly proclaimed their African roots and thereby their Kenyan identity, in the newly independent Kenya, a country struggling to identify itself with either the capitalist or socialist international movements of the time, they seem afflicted of the same disease and simultaneously affirm and repudiate their long fought for identity: "Get this in your head Deepa, he is an African, Papa said. He is not us. [...] What do you mean? What's wrong with an African? I am an African. What hypocrisy!" (p. 206). The relationship between the African-Asians and their chosen nation becomes "a relationship straining for definition" (p. 232), as witnessed by the exchange between Njoroge and Mrs. Lall:

> At least let me have a normal family, where I can see my grandchildren grow up as
> Indians, as Hindus. I had dreams too, of children and grandchildren – whom I can
> […] bring up in our ways. I have nothing against Africans. But we are different. You
> are a brother to my son and daughter, you are their best friend. But a husband for
> Deepa – no, Njoroge (p. 248).

In how many different ways can identity be constructed, seems to be the
question that Vassanji posits here. It is a question on the identity of the postmodern subject; in this case the post-colonial subject. Zygmunt Bauman (1994:
138) summarizes it thus: "Now's identity is flawed: incomplete, shaky, dying
the moment it has been born." And even though Bauman's gaze is directed
towards the subject he calls "the modern man", this subject seems to mirror the
African-Asian subject finding himself in a nation that cannot define itself either;
he cannot stand still long enough to reflect and find himself "because there is no
place to stand still on. Every 'now' melts away and disappears, no 'now' can be
expected to last." (ibid.)

Lall's construction of identity through literal narration of stories ends in
self-doubt; as it should be. Identity abhors permanence. The in-between world
seems to be the only place left:

> Here I was, a young Asian graduate in an African country, with neither the prestige
> of whiteness or Europeanness behind me, nor the influence and numbers of a local
> tribe to back me, but carrying instead the stigma from a generalized recent memory
> of an exclusive race of brown 'Shylocks' who had collaborated with the colonizers.
> […] Black chauvinism and reverse racism were the order of the day against Asians
> (p. 276).

Of course, this in-between world is hardly a place of his own choosing; he has
been placed there by competing discourses: first the colonial discourses that saw
in him neither the native African nor the white settler, and second, by the post-
independence that saw in him a caricature to be tolerated.

Nationalism as a process in the construction of identity

Vikram Lall's story effectively engages in a debate over the reality of what
makes up Kenya's identity and nationhood. The presented discourses on the
nationalist movements before and after independence present an assortment of
characters who question each other's roles, commitments, belonging and in
essence identities. The barriers of ethnicity, class and prestige are presented as
both inviolable and breakable (p. 9). But this is a political act on the author's
side; a defiant giving of voice to a silenced section of society by rewriting their
roles in the struggle to nationhood.

But Vassanji knows that historical recollections are as fallible as the
sanitized myths that make up official accounts of history. That is why Vikram

Lall's accounts and recollections get disrupted and sometimes his perceived memories of events questioned and severally brought into disrepute: was his childhood epitome of gentility, Mwangi, as innocent of Mau Mau involvement as he imagined? Mwangi's own grandson, Njoroge, disavows him of this illusion by informing him, much later in life, that Mwangi did in fact administer oaths to Mau Mau supporters; Kihika, the epitome of Mau Mau dread in his childhood later resurfaces as a bible-toting dishevelled old man, who later gets a government appointment as a DC; the feared colonial Sargent Soames resurfaces as a still feared Inspector in the Special Branch in independent Kenya, as does corporal Boniface, now a Major in the GSU (p. 328). Rushdie sums up this fallibility in the narration thus:

> ...] human beings do not perceive things whole; we are not gods but wounded creatures, cracked lenses, capable only of fractured perceptions. Partial beings, in all senses of that phrase. Meaning is a shaky edifice we build out of scraps, dogmas, childhood injuries, newspaper articles, chance remarks, old films, small victories, people hated, people loved; [...]. (Rushdie, 2010: 12).

Attempts at identity construction are attempts at finding meaning in life. As shaky and fragmented as it is portrayed here, one can only surmise that whatever is produced out of the search through narration may not hold out in a retelling and or rewriting.

But this search for meaning on a personal level translates to the search for meaning on a national level. If those finding themselves within the borders of the newly emerging nation could not pin down an acceptable identity for themselves, then the very nature of that emerging nationhood must also be in question. A nation means a people. What kind of nation comes out of Lall's story? Nationalism does involve a certain level of repression of a group of people in order to champion the rights and identity of another. The process of claiming nationhood means that borders have to be claimed, contested and defended; peoples are in effect included or excluded; a sense of belonging is being created or affirmed, while others are being repudiated. It is, therefore, impossible to delink nationalism (as the search for a sense of national identity) from the construction of or search for a personal identity. As Prof. Yash Pal Ghai noted in his keynote address for this colloquium[1], the process of making a constitution is a nationalist endeavor that must also be looked at as another process in the construction of national, communal and personal identity. This constitutionally sanctioned sense of belonging, however, is a slave to the various voices raised in their own narrations to claim a place in the nation; the cacophony of which drowns those minority voices.

But the people residing within the borders of a nation state cannot and should not be regarded as a "unified interpretive community" (Black, 2000: 92) of any propagated official history, especially where the said history fails to be all-inclusive. Failure of history to be unifying of all the peoples in a nation state inevitably leads to failure to develop an all-inclusive sense of nationhood.

And so while the Kenya of the emergency period did not pretend to lay a claim to nationhood, the post-independence Kenya wants to portray an image of nationhood; and succeeds to a point. But at the point where the personal identity and sense of belonging becomes contested and in dire need of renegotiation, the country also begins to show cracks in its nationhood. It is the failure of the country itself to define its nationhood and thus provide a footing for the others to find their identities.

This failure manifests itself in the failure of the nationalist movements pre-independence. Lall paints a picture of a movement that had all kinds of peoples in its ranks, but which decided to cast a blind eye to these collaborators and perpetuate the idea of it belonging to only one group. The socialist leaning Mahesh, the socialist oriented Indian High Commissioner and even Deepa, who hides Njoroge under her bed during a police operation to flush out Mau Mau sympathizers, are not considered heroes of the cause. The narration surrounding the Mau Mau as a movement of black Africans in Kenya is thus shown in Lall's stories to have been another instrument of exclusion and repudiation of the Asians in Kenya. The disintegration of the nationalist movement after independence and the feeling of betrayal that the fighters encounter exacerbate the failure of the country to find its nationhood.

Furthermore, the tragedies that defined the struggles for freedom in pre-independent Kenya are shown to be tragedies that defined the identities of those whose stories Lall is telling. A case in point is Mr Lall's missing pistol. Later it emerges that Mahesh had stolen it (even though the house servant Amini had to be taken into detention on suspicion), handed it over to the Mau Mau under Kihika who later used it to murder the Bruces, a family friendly with the Lalls. After Lall found out, and having been friendly with Billy and Annie Bruce, he could never bring himself again to love his uncle, in effect severing the family bond that had existed. That familial betrayal by Mahesh is later visited upon him after he is denied re-entry into the country because of socialist and dissident activities. For all his devotion to the nationalist cause, Mahesh had to give up his aspirations of being Kenyan and immigrate back to India.

While the problem of nationalism and nationhood in pre-independence Kenya and as a result the problem of constructing personal and collective identities stemmed from the fact that self-determination is impossible in a colonized state, Lall's story shows that it was the matter of ego and chauvinism that shattered the search for nationhood post-independence. The starkly defined ethnic, class and prestige boundaries that were set by the colonizers reduced the colonized subjects, both of African and Asian origins, to selfish peoples who could only advance selfish agendas, because even these agendas basically followed the boundaries pre-determined by the colonizers; meaning that their sense of identity was also pre-determined by the colonizers. The semantics of nationhood in the colony were restricted to ethnic groupings, with the empire reserving the supremacy in the hierarchy. Undermining this colonial semantic of nationhood seems to have been the underlying goal of the nationalist movement in the pre-independence Kenya; an endeavor that Lall's story portrays to have been later subverted by ethnic chauvinism in the post-independence state.

Where in the pre-independence constellation the colonizers determined the boundaries of belonging, the post-independence Kenya brought forth new constellations that sometime defied the old order and at some other times starkly reaffirmed them. And as the colonial Europeans and colonial-minded Asians were abandoning the country at independence, the newly independent black Africans inherited the chauvinistic and racist tendencies of their former colonial masters. The remaining Asians found themselves in the same position as before; neither belonging within nor without, as Lall puts it:

> [...] We Asians were special: we were brown, we were few and frightened and caricatured, and we could be threatened with deportation as aliens even if we had been in the country since the time of Vasco da Gama and before some of the African people had even arrived in the land (p. 330).

In a constellation that saw the Europeans as the oppressors and the black Kenyans as the oppressed, the African-Asians were left somewhere in the middle. The politics of colonialism had ensured that they belonged to neither end of the spectrum; not for lack of involvement in either end of the spectrum either, as witnessed by the Home Guard Patrols that Mr Lall undertakes in Nakuru or by Mahesh collaborating with the Mau Mau.

Patriotism does not guarantee belonging, as Mahesh could witness. And if ethnic and class chauvinism guaranteed a sense of belonging and provided a sense of identity to a select few, then it definitely neither did support a sense of national community, nor did it help in shoring up the fledgling nationalism which would have borne the much sought after nationhood.

Conclusion: A writer's people

So if, to argue with Satre further, to write for one's age means to reflect aggressively with the intention to change (Satre, 1988: 243), then for Vassanji, the question is: for which age did he write this novel, *The In-Between World of Vikram Lall*? If a novel is taken to be an archival work, but one that redirects the gaze to the dark side of history, then Vikram Lall's narration is meant to provide a missing link in another version of archived materials; namely that of officially sanctioned lore. Vassanji, like any other writer, "had to think about ways of looking and how [these ways of looking] alter the configuration of the world" (Naipaul, 2007: 2), and recast the official myths of nationalism and identity in ways that give voice to those either denied it or too timid to shout loud enough to be heard beyond the cacophony of competing voices.

The intellectual class and the political class being natural enemies, the process of claiming and reclaiming never really stops, as Rushdie succinctly puts it:

> So it is clear that redescribing a world is the necessary first step towards changing it. And particularly at times when the State takes reality into its own hands, and sets about distorting it, altering the past to fits its present needs, then the making of alternative realities of art, including the novel of memory, becomes politicized. [...] Writers and politicians are natural rivals. Both groups try to make the world in their own images; they fight for the same territory. And the novel is one way of denying the official, politician's version of the truth (Rushdie, 2010: 14).

Lall is not denying any official account, nor does he claim a more infallible version; he tells his story, so that his story can be one of the many possible stories that defined and define the Kenyan nationhood. "[...] the writer's task is, [therefore,] to invent – or reinvent – reality, [...] to tell or retell the [history]" (Black, 2000: 92).

Black calls this "a decentered history" (Ibid: 94), meaning that literature does not try to distort the official versions of history but actually illuminate it by incorporating the parts that might have been left out in the official lore.

In a nation still in search of its nationhood, the currency of storytelling goes beyond any one age. And if the world was created by the word, then the Kenyan identity and nationhood can only be realized by telling the many different stories of those that call it home.

Works Cited

Bauman, Z (1994) Desert Spectacular. In K Tester (Ed.), *The Flaneur* (pp. 138–157). London/New York: Routledge.

Black, J (2000) Literature as Secret History. In M Schmeling, et.al. (Eds.) *Literatur in Zeitalter der Globalisierung* (pp. 83-97). Würzburg: Königshausen & Neumann.

Naipaul, V S (2007) *A Writer's People. Ways of Looking and Feeling*. London: Picador.

Rushdie, S (2010) *Imaginary Homelands*. London: Vintage Books.

Satre, J P (1988) *'What is Literature?' And Other Essays*. Cambridge: Harvard University Press.

Schmeling, M et.al. (Eds.) *Literatur im Zeitalter der Globalisierung*. Würzburg: Königshausen & Neumann.

Tester, K (Ed.)(1994) *The Flaneur*. London/New York: Routledge.

Vassanji, M G (2005) *The In-Between World of Vikram Lall*. Edinburgh: Canongate Books.

Whitebrook, M (2001) *Identity, Narrative and Politics*. London: Routledge.

Notes

1. *http://www.star.co.ke/news/2016/07/30/the-law-aims-to-give-every-kenyan-semse-of-belonging_c1394037 Kenya's constitution is about identity in a number of ways. First and foremost, it is about defining our identity as a people. This is stated upfront—in the preamble--where, in the name of the people, the constitution says that we are "Proud of our ethnic, cultural and religious diversity, and determined to live in peace and unity as one indivisible sovereign nation". It commits us to "nurturing and protecting the well-being of individual, the family, communities and the nation".*

5.

The question of identity, dying and death: An analysis of Margaret Ogola's 'Place Of Destiny'

Judith Jefwa

Abstract

Identity remains one of the most central and most contested concepts in circulation today. No individual or group can escape the question of identity in a range of categories be it gender, class, religion, politics nationality or race (Adams, Bennion, and Huh). However, one area that remains relatively neglected in a discussion on identity in works of fiction is that of dying and death. If existence is a question of identity, then death is invariably a question of how people disengage from the identities that they have established in life. This paper argues that to understand one's existence, one must also understand one's end-of-existence. Death is a point of change in relation to identity. The purpose of this paper is, therefore, to examine how fiction depicts the manner in which human beings disengage from their identities.

Michel Foucault argues that artistic works can help address matters pertaining to identity and death because writers' poetic license enables them to capture what may appear to be difficult to capture in real life, through a method known as transgression. Creative writers are able to make the dying and death the canvas upon which they explore the question of identity. This paper intends to use Margaret Ogola's Place of Destiny to explore Ogola's presentation of this pertinent issue. It uses James Marcia's (1966) Identity Status Approach to explain the manner in which the protagonist, Amor relates to issues of identity in the face of her impending death.

Introduction

Death is inevitable. It is the major fact of life that one can predict with certainty that it will come to pass. All through the ages, people have tried to understand death as well as its implication on human life. Societies have established belief systems that address the issue of how people should live in recognition that death is inevitable. People are also taught within their cultures how to handle the grief that comes with death. Elizabeth Bronfen and Sarah Webster Goodwin address the centrality of death in life when they say that 'much of what we call culture comes together around the collective response to death' (3).Their observation indicates how the perceptions that people have of death shape the understanding a culture.

Despite all the sensitisation about dying and death that people get right from childhood and all the way to adulthood, they do not really know how to respond to death. This confusion can be discerned even from the debates that scholars have concerning how people respond to it. For example, anthropologist Earnest Becker believes that there is no single person who does not fear death. He says:

> The idea of death, the fear of death haunts the human animal like nothing else; it is the mainspring of human activity, activity designed largely to avoid the fatality of death, to overcome it by denying in some way that it is the final destiny of man. (ix)

This means that the fear of death is a recognized response to dying and death. Sigmund Freud, Andrew Schopp and Kathy Charmaz, on the other hand, have suggested that the most significant response to dying and death is denial. Freud says that 'at the bottom, no one believes in his own death'. In other words, unconsciously 'every one of us is convinced of our mortality' (305). Schopp, in *The Encyclopedia of Death and Dying*, suggests that the fear of death is not the only response to dying and death, because modernization and civilization allow humanity the space to imagine that they have power over life and death (3). Charmaz augments Schopp's argument by saying that the modern life gives people 'the illusion to self-sufficiency' (14). Friedrich Nietzsche in *Thus Spoke Zarathustra*, suggests that people in some cases embrace death and suffering and thus rise above the rest who are afraid of it or go into denial.

If awareness of death is a major fact of life, why then do people deny its existence? Why are they so afraid of it? One response would be that, phenomenologically, life is about being. It entails activity, purpose, and a creation of various identities within the political, social and religious spheres of life. Death is thus an antithesis of life. People having established identities within their worlds often find it difficult to disengage from these identities and roles that they play in society.

What then is the view of creative writers concerning how people respond to death and dying? Generally, issues pertaining to this phenomenon are traditionally thought of as concerning mainly religion, medicine and anthropology. However, this paper establishes itself upon the belief that literature provides the best space to critically examine very closely how people generally respond to matters pertaining to dying and death but more specifically to the manner in which they treat their exit from the world and the identities that they have created over time. Literary works have the capacity to examine a people's experiences, values, and attitudes in a much deeper and extensive manner. The creative power inherent in literature provides literary artists with the license to present even that which cannot be openly discerned by individuals. Thus literature offers a different insight into responses to death and dying different from that of medicine, anthropology, and religion. Literature also affords people the opportunity to examine and critique what the writers have presented as their views of society and more importantly, it affords people the opportunity to compare different writers' views of this topic. According to Michel Foucault, artistic works are so versatile that they are able to capture what may appear to be difficult to capture in real life, through a method known as transgression. Through transgression, creative writers can go beyond the limitations of life. Foucault says that 'writing unfolds like a game that inevitably moves beyond its own rules and finally leaves them behind' (qtd. in Gutting 22). Creative writers, because of the strategies of transgression, are able to make the dying and death the canvass upon which they explore the manner in which people die in which people respond to death. They are not only able to portray the outward aspects of the individual, but also interrogate what goes on in the mind.

They go beyond the natural and are able to deal with issues which one cannot possibly discern in the day to day world. In this way, this study has been able to capture the artistic presentations of how people deal with death, a phenomenon that is not only traumatic but also elusive. Bisi Ogunsina points out that literature not only transmits ideology, but is also an active creator of meaning. This means that literature does not simply present reality, it also reconstructs reality. In this case, the writer uses available writing techniques to direct the readers towards confronting the limitations of the human form. This paper, by focusing on Margaret Ogola's *Place of Destiny*, identifies how characters respond to disengagement from their identities and how they respond to death and dying as a way of ascertaining the general human being's responses to this phenomenon. To determine the nature of these disengagements, this paper focuses on the characters' disengagements from family and professional spaces.

Place of Destiny is about the dying and eventual death of Amor, a mother and wife in the Mwaghera family set up and owner of the Amor Innovative Skills Consultants. In Ogola's other novels, including *The River and the Source* and *I swear by Apollo,* many of the characters die without exposing the characters' feelings in the face of death. In *Place of Destiny,* however, the depiction of the main characters dying is not only as a stylistic device, but is also an ideological statement about the responses to dying and death in general. Considering that Ogola wrote this novel at almost the same time as she was facing her imminent death from cancer, one can infer that she was using her own experiences to make a definitive statement about how she believed people should live and how they should handle dying and death.

A reading of various works of fiction reveals the extent to which people find it hard to disengage from the life they have lived. In Leo Tolstoy's *The Death of Ivan Ilych,* Ivan Ilych cannot believe that he is dying. He believes that his status in life should protect him from the vulgarities of life. He also believes that it is only other people, whom he refers to as Caius, who should die. In Efua Sutherland's *Edufa,* Edufa does not feel ready to die, and so he visits a diviner and receives a charm that will enable someone else to die for him. It is bait that his wife Ampoma, unwittingly, takes and ends up dying from an undisclosed illness that comes upon her once she promises to die for Edufa. One can also argue that King Lear in Shakespeare's *King Lear* goes through a similar fear and denial of dying and death. He is old and nearing his death. To cushion himself against the vulgarities of life, he opts to abdicate his throne, and then divide his lands among whichever of his three daughters, Goneril, Regan, and Cordelia would flatter him most. He hopes that he can live through his children.

From the foregoing, one can clearly see that creative writers have presented characters' responses to death as emanating from the fear they have of disengaging from their identities. One reason why people fear death is that it strikes as a time when they least expect it to. In a number of works of fiction, characters facing death are depicted as not being ready for it. They are presented as not having taken time to consider and prepare for it. However, in *Place of Destiny,* the main character is a woman who quickly accepts that she is dying and is equally ready to disengage from the identities that she had created in life. James Marcia's Identity Status Approach can be used explain the manner in which Amor relates to the issues of identity in the face of her impending death.

In his Identity Status Approach, Marcia identifies two dimensions in the process of identity formation. He refers to the first one as exploration and refers to the second one as commitment. Exploration involves 'an active consideration of alternative possible identity elements in a quest for a more complete sense of self, whereas commitment represents a decision to adhere to a specific set of goals, values and beliefs, whether self-initiated or adapted from others' (Scwartz et al. 505). From these two dimensions, Marcia derives four identity statuses or behavior related to identity. He argues that someone who commits to a given way of doing things following a period of relatively intense exploration is categorized as *Identity Achieved.* A person who is still in the exploration process, and who therefore is uncommitted to any recognizable ideology, is said to be in *Moratorium* status. An individual who commits to a set of particular identity elements without having explored alternatives is in the *Foreclosure* status. Finally, a person who is without identity commitments and who is not engaged in exploration is said to be *Identity Diffused*. Based on these four categories, this paper argues that Amor is at the Identity Achieved Status. An analysis of her reaction to her dying status will reveal as much.

To a large extent, Ogola presents death as part of the natural cycle of the journey of life. However, she acknowledges that death often catches people unawares. She thus develops her story from a common trajectory in which people are forced to confront life threatening disease that suddenly cut lives short. Amor, the protagonist in *Place of Destiny*, is suddenly forced to confront the fact that she is dying of liver cancer. Amor's response to the fact that she is dying makes me argue that she is in the Identity Achieved status. This is because Ogola presents her as a progressive protagonist who has had time to think not just about life, but also about death.

Ogola depicts her as a woman who has not been afraid of facing any challenges that life brings her way. For example, she manages to overcome the challenges that girls and women face as a result of the negative and deadening impact of gendered roles that favour boys more than girls. Despite having to handle many chores at home while her brothers are given lighter chores, she still goes ahead and acquires a 'Master's degree in Business Administration and a post-graduate Diploma in Human Psychology' (17), both of which she gets while working and raising a family. She also manages to set up a flourishing business enterprise without the help of her husband. Amor thus manages to beat the patriarchal structures that have always regarded women as inferior to men, by ensuring that she runs her business independently from her husband and making a substantial amount of money in the process. Amor is thus an empowered woman with a great future ahead of her. Despite these achievements, she is suddenly confronted with her impending death. Although initially Amor is thrown aback by the diagnosis, her next move shows that she is still in control of the situation.

One thing that makes Amor remain in control is that dying and death is not something that she is just beginning to contemplate about. Previously, in her healthy life, she had thought about her demise and had even drawn a will. Writing a will shows her acceptance of the limitations of the human form. Amor's argument is that people must plan, not just for the life that they are living, but also plan for life after their deaths. Amor says that she wrote her will 'sometime ago when death was still very remote and of merely theoretical interest' because she is a fastidious person (32). Having acquired quite some wealth in her journey of life, she realises quite early in life that she needs to write a will. She did that and now at the time she is facing imminent death, she only pulls it out to simply update it.

As she brushes up on her will, Amor highlights key aspects of life and will making. First, she argues against traditions that prohibit people from thinking about death. Such traditions obviously, discourage the writing of wills. She says:

> I wanted to prove that I was not only an enlightened woman, but also in charge of
> my life and by inference not afraid of death. Tribal lore has it that if one deliberately
> thinks of, speaks of, to say nothing of writes of, an evil, it would surely become
> incarnate and therefore harm so intrepid and foolish a person. (32)

In many traditional patriarchal societies it is men who write wills because it is believed that the property in the homes belongs to them. In the modern world, however, both men and women draw up wills sometimes independently. Even though Amor has a husband, she does not engage him in her will writing process. We have noted that from the onset, Amor has charted her journey of life by pursuing wealth creation independent of her husband, something she had determined to do right from the beginning of her marriage. In terms of economic pursuit, she abandons a collective approach and sees the world as place where individual efforts and freedom have to be respected. That freedom includes choosing how to distribute the wealth that accrues from this individual enterprise. Nonetheless, Amor warns against lust for money as well as excessive materialistic tendencies that make people overspend on luxuries. She says:

> I will not dwell on the great evils that have been committed by people who lusted
> over money above all else, above reason and about life itself....I will not even
> whisper a word about those idiots who spend their hard-earned cash to prop up an
> expensive and ostentatious life style even if it gets them into eternal debt. (33-34)

According to Amor, indolence, greed and unaffordable and expensive lifestyles result in debt-ridden lives that are not family friendly. Thus, in order to ensure the growth of family, the journey of life requires that one adheres to a consistent policy of wealth creation and wise spending, so that at the end of one's life, one can have a significant amount of wealth to bequeath to his or her next of kin. Wealth creation, therefore, empowers individuals and families, because it cushions them when death strikes. Wills on their part give dying people the opportunity to put their minds at rest. Will writing is not only an indication of an enlightened mind it is also a tool of empowerment.

Through Amor, Ogola also argues that writing wills make people give reality a second look. It makes them consciously accept that they will be absent from a future that they are charting out.

However, this does not mean that others will not be around to advance that future that the individual is charting out in the present. Wills are thus written by people to ensure that they have a semblance of control over a future that they may not be present in. In other words, wills are, to a great extent, recognisable power control tools. Yet, because wills require the good will of other people for them to be successfully implemented, dying people have to respect those significant others that they expect to handle the will. Works of fiction can be used to illustrate this. In Gabriel Marquez 'Big Mama's Funeral,' the challenges of ensuring a proper execution of Big Mama's will is that that she does not have the good will of her family. In *Sense and Sensibility* by Jane Austen, Henry

Dashwood dies, leaving all his money to his first wife's son John Dashwood. Henry leaves very little money to his second wife and her three daughters, but asks his son John to take care of them. John promises to do so, but immediately Henry dies, John's mother moves into the home and they ignore Henry's request to take care of the rest of the family. In this case, there is lack of goodwill on the part of John.

The situation is different in *Place of Destiny*. While accepting that she is dying, Amor still hopes that the firm which she has painstakingly taken time to build up will continue to thrive even when she dies. She believes that this is only possible if she empowers those people whom she will leave behind. Although she wills the firm to her only son, Pala, she realises that he cannot handle the company at all because he is still very young. Thus, she ensures that the firm is left in the hands of her faithful employees. She hopes that the positive relationship that she has had with her employees will ensure a smooth running of the company when she finally dies. She gives her employees an opportunity to buy into the company so that as part owners they can feel an obligation to run the company effectively. She tells her employees that with the help of her lawyers, she has had to make a few adjustments to her will 'which will put the company in more hands than while leaving the slight majority in the hands of [her] family' (99). She then gives them the opportunity to buy into the company so as to 'take it where [they] want it to be' (99-100). In so doing, Amor recognises that in the journey of life, the power of the collective in advancement of individually-founded enterprises is very important. It also shows an acceptance of the limitations of what humans can do as individuals. If a company or enterprise is run by one person, when that person dies, it might spell the downfall of the organisation. Although there are situations where many organisations have crumbled when a person dies and leaves it to a group of people, Ogola seems to be of the opinion that if such enterprises are left to handpicked individuals who understand the worth of the organisation, the possibility of the company crumbling is very low. This is probably why Amor carefully selects Ithoth Kela and Lanoi Sompesha, her two trusted employees, as the people to run her firm when she is gone. Her decision to allow other people to run her organisation shows that she has accepted the fact that she dying.

Although Amor indicates that her desire is to leave her company to Pala, she expects Pala to work hard to get the position. For Amor, getting the benefits of a will is not automatic. Her son and her daughters have to work hard and show good reasons as to why they should benefit from her wealth. In this respect, Amor underscores the value of hard work as a part of life and as a response to death. Amor views power over death as emanating, not from money, but from the hard work that goes into wealth creation. The wealth that is then bequeathed to individuals can only be beneficial to the individuals if they continually work hard in order to create more wealth. Amor, on the other hand, encourages her children to be independent-minded so that they can do things for themselves, instead of being dependent on others for economic security. Because she knows that her employees and her children are individually hardworking and honest people, she does not have to worry about the future of her firm when she is gone. This makes acceptance of her death easy.

Amor works at her acceptance to disengage from her roles and identity through a sense of rationalisation and then acceptance. After realising that her end is inevitable, Amor begins to justify why it is alright for her to die. She says that her dying is justified because she has lived a good life and has very little reason to complain. She says that she has had 'deep and fulfilling relationships...money from a successful though stressful career [and] joys and the occasional anguish of motherhood...[and] having known happiness'(17-18). Ogola presents Amor as an open minded character who is able to achieve a high level of flexibility that enables her to appreciate that life has both the good and the bad. Rationalising enables Amor to transfer her libidinal energies from the pain of knowing that she is dying to recognition of the advantages that life has allowed her to enjoy. Through her rationalisation, she is able to become the strongest member of the family even though ideally, she should be the weakest. Thus rationalisation gives her the power to control the people around her and the dying process. At this point in her emotional journey, rationalisation strengthens her into an acceptance of aspects of her life that she has no control of.

She recognises that in her previously well life, she could control her academic pursuits, her career growth and the management of her family members and staff members. In her dying state, she realises that she has to shift control to the dying process so as to ensure that she dies with ease. Accepting that her death is inevitable is the first step towards achieving this goal. This acceptance thus gives her the courage to think of death not as a form of imprisonment, but as a form of freedom. She says, 'I suddenly experience an impatience, a powerful yearning that it might be over and quickly. One moment alive. The next, gone. Free.' (32).

Another thing that makes Amor rationalise her dying is that she takes the blame for having allowed the cancer to have gown to unmanageable levels. Amor is a progressive and practical oriented woman who understands that one of the challenges that people face is finding time to visit doctors in order to get treated for what they consider minor ailments. They only visit doctors when 'the pain is so persistent' (24). Unfortunately, many people often realise that they have cancer or any other terminal illness when it is too late. As in Amor's case, the liver cancer is 'advanced and inoperable' (31). The cancer is detected at such an advanced state that no meaningful treatment can take place.

Through Amor's journey of life, Ogola also appreciates the fact that by its nature, life is 'compelling and exhilarating...[and] even bugs and viruses feel compelled to hang on grimly to whatever version of life they happen to possess' (21). In other words, people are so caught up in the exciting business of living that they never take a moment to reflect on where the business of living ends. Even if they do, they believe that they can overcome death. That is the ontological nature of humans: to believe that they are invincible and immortal. Oscar Maina puts it clearly by saying that 'a careful exploration of human activities surrounding the issues of death and immortality reveals an obsession with the expression of the possibility of defeating death' (187). Freud also argues that humans unconsciously do not accept death because they feel that it devalues them (5).

When Amor compares the human quest for immortality with that of bugs and viruses, the underlying message is that human immortality desire emanates from their base animal instinct. It is in their genetic makeup, which is probably why human beings unconsciously refrain from thinking about their own deaths or planning for their demise. Nonetheless, through Amor, Ogola urges her readers to never 'leave such a question- [the question of dying], perhaps the most important and meaningful question in this life, to the very end'(21). By presenting this view of life, Ogola is challenging individuals to go against their natural self-preservation instincts. She calls on people to move beyond the basic animal instinct, and consciously and intelligently realise that there is no way to escape death.

From the forgoing, it is clear that Amor has had time to think about her life, the roles that she has played in life and the way to disengage from her identity markers. Unlike Ivan Ilych, Edufa and King Lear who can be said to be at the moratorium phase because they are uncommitted to accepting the inevitability of death, Amor is presented as one who is free from experiencing a crisis of identity, since she has had time to appreciate that dying is part of life.

Works cited

Adams, Gerald R, Layne D Bennion, and K Huh. *Objective Measure of Ego Identity Status: A Reference Manual*, Unpublished manuscript. Department of Family Studies, University of Guelph, Guelph, Ontario, Canada N1G2W1, 1989. Print.

Becker, Earnest. *The Denial of Death.* New York: Free Press, 1973.

Bronfen, Elizabeth, and Sarah W Goodwin. 'Introduction' in Elizabeth Bronfen and Sarah W Goodwin eds, *Death and Representation.* Baltimore: Johns Hopkins UP, 1993.

Charmaz, Kathy. *The Social Reality of Death: Death in Contemporary America.* Boston: Addison-Wesley

Freud, Sigmund. 'On Narcissism: An Introduction.' *Standard Edition.* 14. 73-102, 1914.

Marcia, James. E. Development and validation of ego-identity status. *Journal of Personality and Social Psychology*, 3.5, 551, 1966.

Nietzsche, Friedrich. *Thus Spoke Zarathustra.* Eds Adrian Don Caro and Robert B Pippin Trans. Adrian Don Caro. Cambridge: Cambridge UP, 2006.

Ogola, Margaret. *The River and the Source.* Nairobi: Focus, 1994.

Ogola, Margaret. *I Swear by Apollo.* Nairobi: Focus, 2002.

Ogola, Margaret. *Place of Destiny.* Nairobi: Pauline, 2005.

Ogunsina, Bisi. 'Gender Ideology: The Portrayal of Women in Yoruba Ijala.' In *African Languages and Culture.* 9.1. 83-93. 1996.

Schwartz, Seth J, Ronald L Mullis, Alan S Waterman and Richard M Dunham. 'Ego Identity Status, Identity Style, and Personal Expressiveness: An Empirical Investigation of Three Convergent Constructs.' *Journal of Adolescent Research.* 15. 4, July 2000 504-52.

Tolstoy, Leo. *The Death of Ivan Ilych and Other Stories.* St. Louis: Turtleback Books. 2003.

Tolstoy, Leo. *War and Peace.* Ludhiana: Kalyani. 1998.

Shakespeare, William. *King Lear.* G K Hunter, ed. King Lear. London: New Penguin Shakespeare, 1972.

Sutherland, Efua, T. *Edufa.* Longman: London, 1987.

6.

Identity and homecoming in 'The Kitchen Toto' and 'Nairobi Half Life': Confronting the colonial and post colonial Kenya through the film

Lencer Achieng' Ndede

Abstract

This paper, from an Arocentric point of view and guided by post colonial literary criticism, interrogates the two films; Nairobi Half Life and The Kitchen Toto with a view to establish the extent to which governance can redefine human identity. It focuses on how the forces present in the colonial and post colonial Kenyan government divided people in terms of 'us' and the 'other' (colonizer-colonized in The Kitchen Toto and haves and have-nots in Nairobi Half Life)with the process of 'othering' resulting into alienation and loss of identity. It traces the protagonists' conscious struggle and move to relocate themselves from the strictures and imprisoning experiences of 'othering', appraising the protagonist's denial of this alienation in his acceptance of homecoming. Thus the issue the study tackles is that of Kenyans loss, the subsequent alienation from their culture and their own selves and the struggle to reclaim these selves once the realization of that loss is made. Finally the conclusion reveals that the protagonists find their identity and fulfillment in the totality of their religions, culture ancestral heritage and a sense of belonging.

Introduction

Until recently, film in Kenya has been marked by external filmmakers using Kenya as a location to tell their own stories. Today Kenyan films made by Kenyans redefine Kenya; telling Kenyan stories, reflecting the Kenyan life, culture, values and making statements about the Kenyan society. The paper examines *The Kitchen Toto* as a complex cultural, historical and political formation with substantial ties to Kenyan history and to colonial ideology which 'robbed' Kenyans of their identity and defined them as the 'other', and looks at subsequent reclamation Kenyan identity through the struggle for independence. *Nairobi Half Life* on the other hand examines the failure of the postcolonial regime to uphold the principles that drove Kenya to independence: equal opportunities, equal distribution of wealth, jobs and employments among others. It reflects how the post colonial Kenyan government has, again, redefined people in terms of 'us' and the 'other' which has robbed scores of Kenyans of a sense of belonging; 'Us' in the post colonial Kenya being those who belong- in terms of material wealth, and power. *Nairobi Half Life* the move by some Kenyans from rural to urban areas in search of a better life.

Results and discussions

Colonialism played a key role in bringing a sense of alienation and disorder to not only Kenya but also other countries where imperialists ruled. *The Kitchen Toto* speaks extensively about the identity crisis that ensued with colonial oppression. It addresses problems of isolation, frustration and negation of an individual. Through the young Mwangi, the film foregrounds the pain and loneliness Kenyans experienced within the colonial situation. Working on both the individual and the collective levels, the film presents a true picture of life in the colonial Kenya where thousands died either in the hands of colonialists or their fellow Kenyans in an attempt to reclaim their land, dignity and regain their lost identity.

The colonialists assumption of their own superiority, over the original inhabitants of the lands they invaded resulted into an an identity loss for their subjects. The colonialists believed that only the European culture was civilized, sophisticated and 'metropolitan'. While the natives were savage, barbaric, backward and undeveloped. The colonizers therefore disrupted the customs, religions and morals of their subjects. They saw themselves as the centre around which the rest of the universe should revolve and defined the indigenous Africans as the 'other'. The effect of the 'othering' was to impose western values on the African which lead to a subsequent loss of his African heritage and identity. Their homelessness, alienation and rejection become the motivating factors for homecoming.

Culture and religion entails a community's identity. The colonialists invading the African's culture and imposing Christianity was thus a dislocation and destruction of Africans identity. More than just opening up personal experiences of the characters, *The Kitchen Toto* foregrounds the clash between Kenya and the western world in terms of religion and culture. It is a historical and political story set in the 1950s Kenya when colonization by British government officials was well underway. Kenya in the 1950s was a place of increasing tension and dramatic political, economic, and social changes. During this period, there was a wave of the Mau Mau blowing through Kenya which was by then a British colony. Conflicts between the emergent Mau Mau and the colonialists were fast developing, their seeds being in the colonial pattern of social and economic developments. Kenyans' political disillusionment gave way to series of conflicts which gave rise to the Mau Mau uprising. It all begun with a conference which was convened in Berlin in 1884-1885 to partition Africa in an attempt to settle the territorial disputes arising from the Congo region and other parts of Africa. The conference ushered in a period of heightened colonial activity by European powers which eliminated or overrode most existing forms of African autonomy and self-governance. East Africa was consequently divided into territories influenced by European powers and Kenya became a British colony. The British government founded the East African protectorate in 1885 and soon after opened the fertile highlands to white settlers. This was followed by cruel evictions of the Africans from their lands to give room for the white settlers. The Africans thus lost their land to the white settlers and became squatters in their own land. In October 1947 for example, the colonial government brutally evicted African squatters from the olenguruone settlement scheme and forcefully settled them at the semi-arid Yatta region of Machakos. The Africans lost houses, livestock and unharvested crops. Poor living and working conditions followed as the landless Africans were now forced to work for the Britons in their farms in order to raise money to pay taxes to the government. Working on the white farms was not fun either; the Africans working on the farms were mistreated. They had pathetic living and working conditions in the white settler farms where they provided labour; their huts were dilapidated, they wore tartars and although they were provided with food, it was usually posho (maize), as a result they suffered malnutrition and were severely punished at the slightest excuse and even killed by their employers. On 5th sept 1947, for example, a number of African workers were massacred following a strike at the uplands Bacon factory which provoked the urge of retaliation. The killers were not punished.

The Africans were further forced to endure harsh colonial economic policies such as taxation, forced labour and low wages which were oppressive to the Africans who suffered heavily under these policies. Besides the Europeans missionaries condemned the African cultures as being barbaric, backward and savagely. One of these cultures was the female circumcision among the people of central Kenya which created resentment among the natives and roused deep hostility. Furthermore the Africans suffered racial discrimination in their own land. The discrimination extended to the African ex-soldiers who took part in world War II and came back to nothing while their white counterparts were rewarded by being given lands; from which blacks were evicted. These changes, among others, set the stage for the Mau Mau uprising. When the uprising begun, it got support from the urban unemployed Africans, many who were disillusioned World War II ex soldiers. The officials of the central committee coordinated the movement while also organizing for oath taking. The oath was mainly for two reasons: first to ensure that the members remained loyal and honest and could be relied on to keep the secret of the movement and secondly to inspire courage and unite the members to one cause. Betrayal of the oath would lead to instant death and any contrary behavior was dealt with harshly by the Mau Mau.

The Kitchen Toto enters deeply into this drama of conflicts in the 1950s Kenya, with the conflict between the colonialists and the Mau Mau and conflicts amongst the natives being the riding force that propels the plot. The focus of the film is not on the violence by the Mau Mau but the socio-economic and political scenario paralyzing the Kenyan situation at the time. The film conjures a densely woven tale of hidden agendas, betrayal and sacrifice, that is both a deeply personal story and emblematic of the problems that Kenya went through in its struggle for freedom. Through the horrifying dilemma of the young Mwangi, viewers witness the plight of thousands of Kenyans who were trapped in the crossfire of a brutal struggle that would eventually claim several lives. The film lays bare the flipside on whites' high society world and makes a powerful statement about racial inequality and social injustices associated with colonialism. It reveals how Europe's struggle to control the 'New World' came with plundering of both natural and human resources leaving the natives of the 'New World' poor. While the whites lived in affluent houses, colonial ideology of white superiority and black inferiority subjected the natives to poverty and pathetic living conditions. In *The Kitchen Toto*, Bwana John's workers; the natives, do not share the mansion with their white master, they live in a separate mud walled thatched hat with huge gaping holes. They have no furniture and are forced to spend the night on the floor with nothing to cover themselves with. The 'servants' quarters' is nothing but a space to lay one's head.

Through the young Mwangi, the film enables the viewers to enter into the natives' minds to understand the devastating effects of the social conditions the natives were subjected to by the colonialists. Mwangi becomes a kitchen toto (a native young servant) at a very tender age after his father is murdered by the Mau Mau, who later force him to take an oath to liberate his country from colonialism. As a Kitchen toto, he is subjected to endless racism by the whites. Mwangi is caught with failure, inadequacy, shame, and fear pervading his life. He lacks any control over his own existence or direction. He feels trapped inside himself, unable to acknowledge the misery he feels without risking his job which his family depends on. He feels helpless that at his age and having already been circumcised he cannot do anything to help himself and his family. When these feelings; of shame and fear overwhelm him, he lashes out with the only weapon at his disposal; hatred-confirming the whites' definition of Africans as savages. A day after Mwangi spent a night in the cold forest tied to a tree by one of the white settlers; the Grahams go for a picnic and take with them

Mwangi and the servants to serve snacks and drinks. When Mwangi sees the white man who tied him to a tree for allegedly trace passing into his territory, he spits in the sandwich before he serves it to him. Through the young Mwangi's action, viewers can learn that even the Mau Mau militants were not born violent criminals. They are products of social injustices of the British colonial system and the racism that suffuse it. The innocent Mwangi's mind turns to hatred after he is subjected to inhuman treatment by the Whiteman. The exploration of the young Mwangi's psychological corruption gives a new perspective on the oppressive effect colonialism and the subsequent racism had on the black population in the 1950s Kenya. Their psychological damage resulted from the constant barrage of colonial ideologies and the racial oppression they faced. The blacks lived in cramped and squalid conditions, enduring socially enforced poverty and having little opportunity for success. Their resulting attitude toward whites was a volatile combination of powerful anger and powerful fear. Mau Mau was thus a product of the colonial system. They conceived of "whiteness" not as individuals but as an overpowering and hostile force set against them and that had to be overcome. As such they did everything they could to fight the colonialists. This included 'forcing' their fellow blacks to take oath of secrecy and union against the white man and mercilessly punishing any betrayal. It is on these grounds that Mwangi's father, a clergy man, and Mugo, the white police commandant's cook are brutally murdered. Mwangi's father, is murdered for preaching against taking of 'thenge' oath and asking his congregation to denounce the oath while Mugo is hanged for failing to behead the white police commandant. The Killing of a white man or his black collaborators does not evoke guilt in the Mau Mau. Their brutal murder of Mwangi's father and the subsequent torching of his home and later the murder of the cook are both brutal and cold blooded. The film does not spare any of these gruesome cruel details nor does it bring out the Mau Mau as traditional heroes. Instead the film emphasizes the extreme pain and rage the Mau Mau feels which make them capable of such terrible acts as murdering their own in cold blood. By explicitly showing the brutal acts, the film shows that the Mau Mau are not a moral innocent. They are not presented as people to be admired, but as frightening and upsetting figures created by colonialism. Given the social conditions in which the blacks must live, the Mau Mau are what one might expect them to be—violent, hateful, and resentful; made by the colonialism. Confronted by racism and oppression and left with very few options in their lives, these men displayed increasingly antisocial and violent behavior, and were, in effect, disasters waiting to happen. The film illustrates the ways in which white racism forced blacks into a pressured, and therefore dangerous, state of mind.

The conflict between Africa and the west due to colonialism alienated the Africans from their cultural roots and their own identity. In *The kitchen Toto* colonialism coupled with Christianity dislocated Kenyans from the realities of their cultural and religious historical experiences. Blacks were beset with the hardship of economic oppression and forced to act subserviently before their oppressors. In Africa masculinity is divine and gender hierarchy was in such a way that men held a superior position to women. Gender roles were clearly defined and men were considered heads of families while women carried out domestic chores such as cocking, fetching water etc. In such a society a man cooking and serving a woman is a humiliation too grave. In *The Kitchen Toto* colonialism reduced fully grown circumcised kikuyu men like Mugo and Mwangi to cooking for a woman and serving her tea in her bedroom; a psychological humiliation too deep to bear. Given such conditions, it becomes inevitable that the blacks will react with violence and hatred. The Mau Mau movement was thus instinctive and inevitable.

The destruction of the means to self esteem and identity, as seen through Mwangi, left some Kenyans at cross roads. Mwangi is alienated and the confusing experience of mixing the two cultures incapacitates him. He is thrown in to confusion by the west imposing its culture on to his African culture. He is trapped between these conflicts unable to decide whether to place his loyalty with the British whose money supports his family or with the Kikuyu rebels, the people of his tribe. At one point he assists the Mau Mau to escape when they are rounded by Mr. Graham's soldiers, at another he tries to save Mrs. Graham from the Mau Maus and later attempts to save Graham's baby. His indecision proves fatal; he dies in the hands of his own master having been rejected by both his master and the people of his tribe. Through this, the film metaphorically describes a sense of loss which eventually alienated and estranged Kenyans from their culture. The colonized people thus ended up having conflicts with themselves. The Mau Mau therefore thus decided to resolve this dilemma by making an arduous pilgrimage that would liberate Kenya from the alienating influences of the new culture.

The "initiation" in to the new culture and new identity as 'civilized' was a painful experience for the Africans. For Mwangi, he had to be scrubbed and disinfected before being ushered into 'civilization'. For a 12 year old circumcised Kikuyu boy to be bathed naked in full view of everyone including a white woman was a great humiliation. It was the price he had to pay to be forgiven his blackness. As he is scrubbed "clean" he cries out of shame and humiliation. The humiliation he endures makes him aware of how powerless the Africans are under the white colonial rule. The knowledge of his family's situation does not allow him to rebel and run away from the humiliation to which the colonialist subjected him. All he can do is cry. His tears and the new attire become the symbols of the pain involved in losing his original identity for a new identity. Thus Kenyans painfully got a new identity in the process losing his original identity and religion. It is this pain that triggers his realization that he has to reclaim his true self, thus he has to fight against the alienation engendered by his sojourn in the new culture and return to her ancestral experiences and true identity. The Mau Mau thus made a strong statement seeking a return to their Africanness. The Mau Mau rebellion thus was a cry of fulfillment and a relocation from the strictures of colonialism which alienated the Kenyan from his own self and cultural identity and reality of his ancestral people.

The Mau Mau's struggle for independence in *The kitchen Toto* is a motif of homecoming. Upon realization that Christianity is responsible for Kenyans' alienation from their identity culture and land, the Mau Mau attempts to reclaim their true selves by fighting against the alienation. and return to their reality. They attempt to make a fulfillment within the cultural and religious sphere of their ancestral people by administering a traditional oath. In strong terms, the Mau Mau's rejected and denied the colonialists' superiority and struggled home to their own identity and tradition. They fought Christianity and colonialism which was the source of their alienation and which underlined the cultural forces out to destroy their cultural identity.

Nairobi Half Life

Nairobi Half life foregrounds how the post colonial Kenyan government has 'redefined' people in terms of us and the other; 'us' being those who belong; in terms of material wealth, power and 'correct tribe'. Understanding of Kenya's colonial history is necessary in understanding the present day Kenya. In 1963, Kenya gained its independence from the British and effectively became a republic the following year. The country's first president, Jomo Kenyatta, a Kikuyu, took over property that belonged to wealthy white settlers and redistributed it amongst Kenyans, favoring the Kikuyu in particular. Although he claimed that the country had achieved "political stability" by strengthening its economy through tourism and other reforms, underlying social tensions between the Kikuyu and other minority groups remained. After independence there was rapid population growth, combined with the migration of people from rural areas to the cities, which contributed to high rates of unemployment as well as lawlessness and disorder in urban areas. In 1978, after Kenyatta died, Daniel arap Moi began his infamous 24-year siege of power. Over the subsequent decades, economic growth declined and dropped under 4%, a dramatic drop from the growth rate of 6% during the early years of Kenyatta's presidency. According to Robert Shaw, a Nairobi economist quoted by the BBC, "From the 1990s, economic growth and the standard of living have declined or stagnated.... Moi's government promised many things but did very little – especially in the department of good governance." As a result, many families fell below the poverty line, and the economic stagnation contributed to an already growing dissatisfaction aggravated by government inefficiency, corruption and ethnic tensions. The said Kenya's post colonial disillusionments set the stage for the themes foregrounded in *Nairobi Half Life.*

Set in 2012 Kenya, the film majorly deals with the twin theme of crime and violence. This is attributed to the fact that the prevalence of crime and violence in postcolonial Kenya parallels a history of crime and violence that is generally attributed to the youth in postcolonial Africa. According to Tom Odhiambo (2007): The prevalence of juvenile delinquents in their works and the related acts of violence and criminality could be read as indictors of the failure of the postcolonial Kenyan State to 'include' their young men (and women) into the mainstream of society— there is a correlation between marginalization of the youth in society and their adoption of anti-social behavior as strategies to access material resources (134). Richard Cloward and Lloyd Ohlin suggested that delinquency can result from differential opportunity for lower class youth. Such youths may be tempted to take up criminal activities, choosing an illegitimate path that provides them more lucrative economic benefits than conventional, over legal options such as minimum wage-paying jobs available to them. Criminal activities thus become 'imaginary solutions' to the problem of belonging to a subordinate class.

Nairobi Half Life examines the failure of the postcolonial regime to uphold the principles that drove Kenya to independence: equal opportunities, equal distribution of wealth, jobs and employments among others. In the film, the rural folks have been left behind in terms of development, as a result they move to the cities in search for a better life making the cities crowded, in turn lack of jobs and proper housing sets in. As the city gets more and more crowded, lawlessness sets in and the police fail to maintain law and prevent crime; they instead take part in crime by protecting the criminals. The film seems to be asking a philosophical question "What happens when the criminal is not the 'enemy without', but the regime itself"

The film is an allegory of the post colonial Kenya, with the main character representing the rural folk and their move towards the city of lights in search of better life, revealing the problems inherent in the post colonial governance. It represents societies that have recently emerged from colonialism and describes the way these societies function in the post- colonial order. The film foregrounds the fact that though imperialism has passed and the colonies have attained an independent status, these nations of the third world face a lot of economic, social and political problems such as bad governance, rural-urban migration, corruption, poverty, crime and violence, among others. The themes in *Nairobi Half Life* reflect the predicament of man in the present day cities. It throws light on the Post- colonial and post- imperial realities that have shaped the contemporary societies and provides important insights relating to them leading to a better understanding of the problems that are faced by the post- imperial generations.

The film deals with crime in the Kenyan urban areas and argues that crime can be learned through association. Interacting with antisocial peers is a major cause of criminal behaviour in the society. When criminal subcultures exist, many individuals can learn associatively to commit crime and crime rates may increase in those specific locations. Mwas, an innocent young man aspires to become an actor. Obsessed by his quest to become an actor, he sets out to the city of opportunities; just like many young stars who see Nairobi as a city of opportunities. He is robbed of all that he had just as he lands in the 'City of Lights'. Confused and distraught, after his robbery, he paces aimlessly along the city and lands in the hands of the Nairobi city council officials, who mistakenly arrests him and throws him in the police cell for allegedly hawking. While in the police cell, he meets Oti, one of Nairobi's street smart gang members who introduce him to his gang upon leaving central police. As Mwas lives with Oti and his gang, he learns about the crime culture in Nairobi thereby becoming a criminal by association. Mwas becomes so perfect that he even initiates his small snatch and run gang into car-jacking and robbery with violence.

In the film, Nairobi city is shown as more complicated than an outsider might assume. The film gives a discourse of Nairobi city showing how social and economic conditions can reinforce crime culture in the society. Societal factors such as poverty are shown to predispose people to crime. Those who fail to get employment find refuge in the hands of other jobless Kenyans. The film depicts the disastrous effects poverty has upon the society. It shows how poverty in the land reflects on the mind. It exposes men's vulnerability in the face of poverty leaving them desperate, absurd, resigned to fate, low self esteem, and loss of social order. The effect of poverty manifests itself in behaviours such as adoption of deviant sub cultural norms which may include toughness and disrespect for authority. Criminal acts may result when youths conform to norms of the deviant subculture. Albert K. Cohen (1997) in sub cultural theory suggests that delinquency among lower class youths is a reaction against the social norms of the middle class. Some youths, especially from poorer areas where opportunities are scarce, might fragment away from the mainstream to form their own values and meanings about life. Finding life difficult in Nairobi, Oti and his friends form a sub-group which specializes in stealing motor vehicle spare parts. While the men try to survive by becoming criminals, the girls go to an extend of 'selling' themselves for as low as 20 shillings so as to earn a living.

As Mwas continues living in the poverty stricken crowded slum with his gangster friends, morality becomes increasingly ambiguous and complex. Through Mwas' life in the city the film suggests that in a world complicated by poverty, and a failed system, it is not simple to identify right and wrong. Mwas's actions do not represent a moral action; by all standards he is a criminal. However, though a criminal the film imply that he is not fully to blame for his actions. Though Mwas make a conscious choice to join Oti and his gang thereby becoming a criminal, the mindset in which he makes these choices has been shaped by the social structure; poverty coupled with desperation that the society help to perpetuate. Mwas goes to town an innocent boy in search of his dream of becoming an actor but ends up on the streets miserable, jobless and homeless. Sociological factors such as social services gap between the rural and urban areas contribute to people leaving their rural homes to search for opportunities in the city. Social services facilities such as theatres are located in urban areas and as such for Mwas to become an actor he has to move from his home village to the city. With increase of population in the urban areas comes decrease in employment, housing and transport among others. The resultant joblessness and shuttered dreams provide a fertile ground for criminal activities. The desperation that sets in with joblessness and homelessness coupled with social strain on individuals to achieve upward financial mobility causes those individuals to act out in ways that are illegal when legal means to achieve upward mobility are not available to them. Mwas' gang composes of jobless urban residents whose places in the society are determined by forces almost completely beyond their control. A long-standing unequal division of wealth has trapped them within a disadvantaged class. They lack opportunity to get meaningful employment as Oti says '*hii ni Nairobi huwezi mek bila connection*' This is Nairobi, you cannot make it without connections. Poverty is thus a trap determined by forces almost completely beyond the ordinary citizens' control. Chicago School sociologists adopted a social ecology approach to studying cities, and postulated that urban neighborhoods with high levels of poverty often experience breakdown in the social structure and institutions such as family and school. This results in social disorganization, which reduces the ability of these institutions to control behavior and create an environment ripe for deviant behavior.

Naturally most people buy into the dream of becoming successful, rich and powerful and it becomes a powerful psychological motivation. If the social structure of opportunities is unequal and prevents the majority from realizing the dream, some of them will turn to illegitimate means (crime) in order to realize it. Others will retreat or drop out into deviant subcultures such as gang members, urban homeless drunks and drug abusers. Mwas dreams of becoming an actor, just as Daddy M dreams of living big. He acts out scenes from the movies he is selling until he comes across the vultures; a theatre group from Nairobi, and sets out to Nairobi to achieve his dream. When he ends up on the streets homeless and frustrated in Nairobi, he seeks refuge from a gang who readily accept him. Many times young people who are threatened by their environment, attacked or hurt and need protection often readily find it offered in the street gangs. They then learn the techniques of crime under the tutorage of the gang around them.

Nairobi Half Life depicts a justice system so undermined by corruption that the concept of law and justice holds little meaning. The film examines the post colonial Kenyan criminal justice system and finds it wanting, most notably in how the police handle the criminals. In the first place, Mwasn an innocent boy is jailed by the county council of Nairobi for a 'crime' he does not commit, which succeeds only in turning a well-meaning boy into a menace to society. His well meant journey to Nairobi is ironically reversed when he comes out of the cell a criminal, showing how the society can make criminals out of innocent citizens. The police fail to maintain law and order and instead of apprehending the criminals take part in crime by sharing in the criminals' loot and in turn offering them protection from the law. The police get a percentage of whatever the robbers make. While they protect the criminals, they make untrue identifications to deceive the public about unsolved crime cases as revealed by Oti to Mwas when they are locked up in a secret hideout by the police. This satirizes the police force and shows how in a corrupt system decision can be formed on the flimsy basis of circumstantial evidence and unreliable witnesses. Justice in the post colonial Kenya, then, is shown to be unjust and unable to grasp the truth of the situation. It is also unable to reform the criminal, who is likely to respond to the reinforcement and protection from the police by becoming more of a criminal and further alienating themselves from the society. The likelihood of being caught, through surveillance, police or security guard presence is effective in reducing crime. When criminals see that the benefits of their crime outweigh the cost such as the probability of apprehension, conviction and punishment, their criminality is reinforced. In Nairobi, the police reinforce crime by failing to apprehend the criminals and share in their loot.

Conclusion

The paper has demonstrated that *The Kitchen Toto* and *Nairobi Half Life* mirror the Kenyan society and reflect the destruction of the Kenyan 'identity' by different forms of governance. The films have also traced the Kenyans' subsequent journeys to homecoming upon realization of the alienation and estrangement. Christianity and the western culture presented African religion and culture as backward and unsuitable for the very same societies who had evolved them in *The Kitchen Toto* just as the post colonial government has unequally distributed wealth, leaving some areas out in the development process resulting into a dislocation of individuals from their realities in *Nairobi Half Life*. Homecoming in the two films is a reconstitution of their dislocated selves from the different predicaments they encounter. In making a homecoming, Kenyans during the colonial period struggled to overthrow the white colonialists which act as avenues through which the return to their identity is achieved, while the post colonial Kenyans move from the rural to urban centres for a better life and to have a sense of belonging. Homecoming therefore implies a move towards reclaiming an identity or a sense of belonging.

Works Cited

Cohen, Albert K. *A General Theory of Subcultures [1955]*. na, 1997

Gitonga, T. "Nairobi half life." *Nairobi: One Fine Day Films*. 2012

Hook, Harry. *The Kitchen Toto*. Warner home video France [éd.], 1994

Odhiambo, Tom. "Juvenile delinquency and violence in the fiction of three Kenyan writers." *Tydskrif vir letterkunde* 44.2 2007: 134-149.

Shaw, Clifford Robe, Henry Donald McKay, and Norman S. Hayner. *Juvenile delinquency and urban areas: A study of rates of delinquents in relation to differential characteristics of local communities in American cities.* Chicago: University of Chicago Press, 1942.

7.

Writing for the Kenyan stage from the year 2000: A practitioner's perspective

John Sibi-Okumu

Abstract

This paper is an encouragement to the greater documentation and study in Kenyan academic circles of, in very broad terms, Western style, 'proscenium arch' stage performance in what could be called the 'Theatre of the New Century'. It also argues that, with greater freedom to create historically, the playwright of the present day has a greater responsibility in helping to bring about an anti-ethnic and pro-minority society within a devolved system of government. The paper is offered by a practicing playwright.

Key words: Language, Ethnicity, Stereotyping, Performance, Identity, Censorship.

Introduction

Who is Kenyan and who is not? Are some more Kenyan than others? What characteristics distinguish Kenyan society? What can Kenyans do to make this society a better one? What appreciation do Kenyans have of their history? These are the questions, all to do with the notions of Identity, Belonging and Citizenship, in the Kenyan context, which have largely informed me as a playwright.

The plays

So far, I have written five, original, as opposed to devised, plays which have all had something to do with what I would broadly describe as 'the Kenyan condition since independence'.

The first, *Role Play, a journey into the Kenyan psyche* (2004) was conceived, as its name suggests, so as to have actors playing against racial type, the better to conjure up a panoramic view of the interactions between 'Blacks,' *(Wafrika* in Kiswahili*),*'Whites,' *(Wazungu)* and 'South Asians,' *(Wahindi).*

Thereafter, the satirical comedy *Minister, karibu!* (2007) employed mistaken identity to expose how the 'Big Man Syndrome' has helped to foster a 'top-down' culture of corruption. Peripheral themes were a patronizing 'Western' view of Kenya as part of some homogenous entity called 'Africa' and also religious hypocrisy.

The play *Dinner at Her Excellency's* (2010) was written for radio and it explores the expectations of a sampling of ethnic and racial stakeholders from Kenya's 2010 constitution.

Meetings (2013), my third play written expressly for the stage, was an artistic plea for reconciliation, cautioning against a repetition in 2013, specifically, of the ethnic violence that had followed the general elections of 2007. In *Meetings*, a political activist who had gone into exile after the failed coup in 1982, returns to Kenya towards the end of 2012 together with a young son from an inter-ethnic union, which he entered into during his 30-year stay in the United States. He is obliged to reunite with several ghosts from his past, including the college-mate informer who had first exposed him to scrutiny by the state, and he must come to terms with the imperatives of the moment.

Elements (2013), a monologue, originally written in French, features a female protagonist with Kenyan antecedents, her Indian grandfather having come to Kenya as an indentured labourer to help build a railway inland from Mombasa. She is a celebrated writer who muses on her creative process and the influences upon it of her own life experience, which was blighted by the trauma of incest in her childhood.

Finally, *Kaggia* (2014), inspired by the life of the leftist-leaning, Kenyan politician Bildad Kaggia, invites the audience to query the consequences of the political choices which Kenya has made after independence and whether more could be done to lessen the huge divide between the haves and have-nots.

Background and inspitation

Playwriting was the inevitable progression for me after I had taken on more than 40 roles on stage, since my teenage years. The roles and, indeed, the years in which they were performed, represent milestones in the history of post-independence, western style, proscenium arch theatre performance in Kenya. And where I was not involved as performer, I was a historical witness.

I knew, for example, that James Ngugi, before he became Ngugi wa Thiong'o, had written *The Black Hermit*, the first play in the English language by a Kenyan whilst he was a student at Makerere College in Uganda, in 1963. I did not see but did register the production of Ngugi's 'politically incorrect' *Ngaahika Ndenda (I Will Marry When I Want)* in 1977. The staging of *Ngaahika Ndenda* was to be part of a series of events which eventually led to Ngugi's exile.

I made my acting debut at the National Theatre in 1973, playing 'Romeo' opposite an English 'Juliet'. This was evidence of a persistent attachment to British theatre. In 1975, I was the First Son, playing opposite the late Francis Imbuga, in the inaugural production of *Muntu*, by the Ghanaian Joe de Graft, a play which was later to be degraded, ignominiously, from school text to banned publication. Imbuga was, of course, to write among several others, the epoch-making play *Betrayal in the City*.

In those days our playwrights set their plays in 'a fictitious African country' for fear of being too specific. And we actors, in our attempts at social commentary, had to take part in plays which took place 'Somewhere Else,' in the hope that comparison would be at best, veiled. Examples, from my own experience include Chilean writer Ariel Dorfman's *Death and the Maiden*, about state torture in a Latin American country and Mtwa/ Ngema/ Simon's *Woza, Albert!*, which posits Jesus Christ's second coming to a racially segregated South Africa.

In the not so distant past, the censor held powerful sway in Kenya and, as already suggested, there were dire consequences for those who dared to displease the powers that were. Those who survived those years were challenged to find ways of, in the formulation of Ugandan playwright John Ruganda: 'telling the truth laughingly'. The climate of apprehension and fear was to last until 1997, when certain prohibitive clauses of the Film and Stage Plays Act were repealed, allowing for a welcome expansion of artistic license.

Milestones and taking the process forward

Therefore, when I wrote *Role Play*, first produced in 2004, the giants upon whose shoulders I now walked, had made it possible for me to abandon self-censorship and to set my action squarely in Kenya; to query in the course of it, who had killed Pio Gama Pinto? Tom Mboya? JM Kariuki? Robert Ouko? To evoke the rape of many South Asian women during the attempted coup of 1982. To point to the existence of unflatteringly called *wazungu* 'Kenya cowboys' and 'Kenya cowgirls' and, in so doing, to remind audiences that the definition of

Kenyan should not always and only be preceded by 'black' as an adjective of colour.

I have evoked four periods in this personal timeline: 1) a period predominated by theatre from the European and especially British tradition; 2) the theatre of the Kenyatta presidency, noteworthy for a flowering of nationalistic plays, largely centred on the theme of tradition versus modernity; 3) the theatre of the Moi presidency, marked, particularly in its latter stages by an acute muzzling of the creative voice and 4) the theatre of the period from the Kibaki presidency to date, with a general resurgence of relatively uncensored artistic activity.

It would stand to reason, consequently, that speaking on behalf of other playwrights; I should be saluting the advent of a creative nirvana. Sadly, not so, on several counts.

Challenges to the practitioner

Most disturbingly, the dark clouds of state censorship seem to be looming over Kenya once again. The language debate has not gone away, either. I find that the recent switch to talking of 'communities' and 'nations' within Kenya represents a great leap backward, because, to my mind, it is as inimical to national cohesion as was talking of 'tribes' in the past. In order that devolution might not become a code word for division, I would argue strongly against plays being written in ethnic languages for ethnic audiences. The use of Kiswahili and English as our self-declared national and official languages, supported strategically over, say, 25 years, would, in my opinion, reap manifest gains for our definition of being Kenyan, as it would make for a form of linguistic unity within cultural and religious diversity.

As a playwright, I have found that simply giving my characters names that pointed to their ethnicity has led to stereotypical and often nefarious assumptions. This is a problem which, I must confess, I am yet to solve to my satisfaction. For example, if my thieving protagonist has a name which sets him out as an El Molo, am I saying to my audience that all El Molos are thieves?

Still on the subject of language, it is also worth noting that great literature displays a mastery of any given language and it is unlikely that national governments will be able to fund the mastery of 40 plus major languages throughout the country, not to mention the mastery of many, distinct dialects. To my mind, it should *not* be part of the national agenda to invest in the preservation of all the languages spoken in Kenya, a project which, understandably, has a strong appeal to those who come from majority groupings. I do believe that our mother tongues *will* survive, simply by continuing to be spoken and written by those many who will continue to rely on them for self-expression, by force of circumstance.

Challenges for academia

My final 'red lights,' as it were, are more direct provocations to the academics among us. It may be true that publishers are loathe to publish plays and poetry because they find little material profit in doing so. Only my first play has been published. But would our universities not consider printing esoteric genres, such as plays and poetry, in limited editions from their own presses? The theatre space has moved forward creatively in different ways but it seems that our intellectuals are keen to sustain the familiar and, perhaps, comforting 'Kenya is a literary desert' debate interminably. I would wager that the social and political concerns of the youth in our lecture halls today are far removed from the concerns which I had as an undergraduate in the early 1970s, when all of them were not yet born. This is a reality which, I would contend, is not sufficiently reflected in our current literary scholarship.

To put it summarily on such a summary occasion and with a nod to William Shakespeare, 400 years after his death: why hold a mirror up to society if there is no desire to look into it?

Conclusion

In conclusion, I would urge our academics to engage more wholeheartedly in taking stock of, analysing and nurturing the creative output for the stage which is now coming from a country which, young as it is in absolute terms, is now more than 50 years old.

Works Cited

Betty Caplan: Role Play. *Daily Nation*, 7 November, 2005.
Ariel Dorfman: *Death and the Maiden*. London: Nick Hern Books. 1996.
Margaretta wa Gacheru: Kaggia. *Business Daily*. 7 November, 2014.
Joe de Graft: *Muntu*. Nairobi. Heinemann Educational Books (E.A.) Ltd. 1977.
Francis Imbuga: *Betrayal in the City*. Nairobi: East African Educational Publishers. 1976.
Kingwa Kamencu: Kaggia. *Saturday Nation*, 8 November, 2014.
Literary Discourse. 'Literature must anchoritself in the past to have a future.' *The Sunday Standard*, 6 November, 2005.
P Mtwa, M Ngema & B Simon: *Woza Albert!* London: Methuen Modern Classics. 2009.
John Sibi-Okumu: *Role Play: A Journey into the Kenyan Psyche*. Nairobi: MvuleAfrica Publishers. 2004
John Sibi-Okumu: *Minister, Karibu!* Unpublished. 2007.

John Sibi-Okumu: *Dinner at Her Excellency's*. Unpublished. 2010.
John Sibi-Okumu: *Meetings*, Unpublished. 2013.
John Sibi-Okumu: *Elements*. Unpublished. 2013.
John Sibi-Okumu: *Kaggia*. Unpublished. 2014.
Khainga Okwemba: Kaggia. *The Star* XXXX DATEXXXX.
George Orido: Kaggia. *The Standard*, 3 November, 2014.
Dana April Seidenberg : Kaggia. *The East African*, November 15-24, 2014.
Ngugi wa Thiong'o: *The Black Hermit*. London: Heinemann. 1968.
Ngugi was Thiong'o and Ngugi wa Mirii: *I Will Marry When I Want To*. Nairobi: East African Educational Publishers Ltd. 1982.

8.

Kenyan-hood, identity and being: Tracing Kenya's identity and belonging in manner of speech and music forms

Kanyi Thiong'o

Abstract

This paper examines the palpability that 'Manner of Speech' and textures of the music and songs that are popular with a given people can aid in understanding a facet of their Identity. An examination of speech patterns common with Kenyans, and the songs Kenyans sing and listen to both local and foreign can reveal aspects of their identity. Drawing from the works of John Austin Speech Act Theory and George Lakoff theory of metaphor, the paper examines practices which a being engages, to constitute the Self, in its constant engagement with music, song, dance and performances as cultural products. Aspects of Self, Identity and Belonging are hereby explored with the aim of understanding how sound sources, as cultural tools govern the self along cultural ideologies whose philosophies continue to act upon the consumers of artistic works but in a way they are not aware. The paper examines the nature of our being that remains subsumed and in most cases unspoken about in artistic forms, which exist not only to articulate the message inherent in a work of art but in addition to construct aspects of our being and Identity. It is hereby argued that songs can be listened to, to try and trace the various shades of our identities that happen to escape our attention mostly as a result of an inability to think of manifestation of ourselves in our music, poetry, performances and narratives. Works of art can be examined to see what they reveal of ourselves, our ideologies, identities and sense of belonging. Good artistes compose their works from the centrality of a clear conscience of their message on one hand and on the other hand with a serious focus on the sensitivity the impact of their style of composition

is likely to have on their audiences, about themselves as audiences and the world around them. Works of art are about human life and human values. The text is a messenger. Examination of styles of song compositions and production can reveal an aspect of our identity and hence the need to develop a style of underpinning audio techniques and the effects they bear upon us. Works of art are emblems of the society that is responsible for their creation. We can, therefore, examine an aspect of the selves in us which is reflected in the artistic works we create or consume. This is of essence in policy making and in moral stock taking of ourselves, if we were to remain relevant as stakeholders in the shaping of our future generation. All artistic works are metaphors, saying something, about something else. The metaphor in the song, in the spoken word, in the performed arts, defines who we are and haunts how we think of ourselves.
Keywords: Identity, Self, Being, Belonging, Speech, Music, Song

Introduction

This article examines the question of Identity, Kenyanhood and Belonging. The paper deviates from the sociological norm of identity construction along ethnic lines and probes a rarely taken approach of examining Kenyan identity(ies) in the people's manner of language and language usages that define aspects of multiple identities of most Kenyans. In this approach the paper takes on a linguistic approach to forge a possible proposition that we can understand Kenyan-ess by critically examining what our manner of speech practices reveal about our unique identities.

The paper argues that to create a more united Kenya we can embark on cultural practices of celebrating the beauty in each others linguistic features aiming to understand and appreciate members of every race or ethnic community by tapping into the beauty of their manner of speech and music forms. To achieve this, the paper argues that we can create a sense of belonging for all Kenyans if we create a positive way of appreciating Kenyans of all backgrounds, if we spare our time to cultivate a mechanism of appreciating the fact that our identity as Kenyans is *multilayered* and that it keeps changing as Kenyans continue to interact with one another and with the world at large. The paper, therefore, argues that identity is not a fixed thing but a dynamic process through which each individual practices *Being*.

The paper in this context examines: identity(ies) in phono-aesthetics, manner of speech and writing and how most Kenyans write can be harnessed to create greater self awareness and of the other. Finally, the paper highlights characteristics of Kenyan music to show how characteristics and patterns of music consumership can be adopted to define a greater sense of belonging for all Kenyans.

Discussion

A historical examination of forms of music, songs and dances that have been popular in Kenya since the pre-colonial era to date reveals the contribution song, music and dances have played in defining Kenyan identities. Songs, music and dances in Kenya have not only served as a source of entertainment but they have played a major role in the development, propagation and popularization of Kenyan identities which have been popular within particular historical epochs. Scholars might not have enthusiastically taken up their role in studying unorthodox cultural phenomena, but popular culture practitioners have actively taken up the work of reflexive self-documentation (Mungai 2008: 57). The categories of songs in the Gikuyu community, for instance, reveal the philosophy and aesthetics that is subsumed in Gikuyu song (Kabira and Mutahi, 1993:20). The artiste in this context is a mouth piece of his or her community. An examination of the different shades and attributes that have formed our identities can be examined by taking a stock of particular themes of self and personhood that define major concerns of music artistes in a given period.

Culture is not static but instead it is always in a state of flux. Our music, songs and dances as part of our culture have also been changing with time. This can be said not only of the music and the respective artistes but the states of our identities as well. This is because music, songs and dances function as emblems of ourselves, our values and ideologies. In tracing our identity, citizenship and personhood, in music, this article adopts Brubaker and Cooper's approach to the study of identity. In this context, identity is conceived as an analytical category. I want to argue that studies on Kenyan identity, personhood and sense of belonging cannot be tied to a particular historical moment, nor can it be examined with a logo centric perspective but instead identity as posited and as our music reveals defines forms of discursive practices. In this context the concept of identity is not a single state of being but it is a condition that exists in multiple forms.

Fearon summarizes identity into the following propositions, to mention a few: 'Identity is people's concepts of who they are, of what sort of people they are, and how they relate to others' (Hogg and Abrams 1988, 2); 'as a description of the way individuals and groups define themselves and are defined by others on the basis of race, ethnicity, religion, language, and culture' (Deng 1995, 1), 'the ways in which individuals and collectivities are distinguished in their social relations with other individuals and collectivities' (Jenkins 1996, 4). 'National identity describes that condition in which a mass of people have made the same identification with national symbols have internalized the symbols of the nation …'(Bloom 1990, 52); 'identity as relatively stable, role-specific understandings and expectations about self' (Wendt 1992, 397). 'Social identities as sets of meanings that an actor attributes to itself while taking the perspective of others, that is, as a social object. And identity as a kind of unsettled space, or an unresolved question in that space, between a number of intersecting discourses. ...[Until recently, we have incorrectly thought that identity is] a kind of fixed point of thought and being, a ground of action ... the logic of something like a 'true self.' ... [But] Identity is a process, identity is split. Identity is not a fixed point but an ambivalent point and the relationship of the other to oneself" (Hall 1989).

As the definitions above reveal the concept of identity operates from an idealized position. It is therefore necessary to question the process through which we define the procedures of self constitution. Kenyan music, song and dances as constitutional frames for constructions of selves can be traced from the role these genres played in the pre, during and post colonial era. In this context music, song and dances have not only functioned to state how we have defined ourselves but the process of performance becomes the agency through which the very construction it posits brings to bear the aspect of the self it purports.

The way everybody speaks is melodious in some way. We however, never take much of our time to record our voices and hear how we sound from the outside. The manner we appropriate sound in speech says much about us and consequently functions to define an aspect of our identity which we carry with us wherever we go. An identity that we use and reaffirm almost every day when we speak, an identity that is known by our listeners but an identity which we ourselves arguably don't know much about. We can trace this identity to take stock of an aspect of our selves, and much more with an aim to learn something about ourselves from the way we speak. As Austin observes,

> To determine what illocutionary act is so performed we must determine in what way we are using the locution: asking or answering a question, giving some information or an assurance or a warning, announcing a verdict or an intention, pronouncing sentence, making an appointment or an appeal or a criticism, making an identification or giving a description, (Austin, 1962: 98)

A refocusing of our voice(s) towards our inner selves may reveal something about us which we never knew and may be it would reveal something about us that we need to work on in order to improve the influence we have on the world around us. We can tell much about people from the way they speak. A voice reveals much more than the speaker's intentions.

One danger this awareness may pose is that some may use the awareness to hide their real selves and hence entangle the society around them in hypocritical discourses without the society's awareness in the judgment the society may pass about the liar as a result of basing as a result of interpreting the speaker in the context of how one sounds. It is however, not possible for an entire society to entangle in the same form of hypocrisy in their manner of speech appropriation. We can however, access the knowledge of how we sound, the melody in our voices to improve our human relations amongst ourselves, with our neighbors and with the world at large.

I want to argue that President Barrack Obama's campaigns as the first Black President of United states for instance were not only successful because of what he was saying but also because of how he used his voice. This convinced the majority Americans to vote for him. Little credit has however gone to the team that is always operating the sound system to ensure that every speech president Obama makes leaves a trace of its power and significance in the minds of the listeners. The timing of the echo, the ratio of the amount of compression, the setting of the release and the attack time which the engineers calibrate to give his voice the effect it has on the audiences functions to refine the quality of his voice for maximum effect in the delivery of the intended message. The beauty of the unprocessed voice which characterizes ordinary uses of our voice is that it is a clear indication of our character, especially when one uses the voice without any conscious intention to modify it. This could mark an element of one's true self. There would then be need to ask the question: 'What does my voice and manner of speech say about me?' 'How do I judge and interpret people as a result of how they sound?' and the bigger question, 'What does our manner of speech say about us as a society?'

Our speech rate may reveal the speed at which we react to situations and hence reveal something about ourselves and our character. Kenya is a state of multiple identities as speech patterns of various ethnic groups may reveal. A focus on cognitive oral linguistic practices of ethnic groups may create better ways of understanding members of each group. This is on the understanding that speech patterns of each group are to be examined in order to reveal their patterns of discerning and cognitive procedures which they employ to construct meaning of themselves and the world's around them. Speech patterns may reveal our temperament and much more about members of a group. An understanding of each group from the revelations of their cognitive processes as evidenced in their speech techniques can help harness our strengths towards better integration and hence build a state whose persons and beings have a sense of belonging. This is on the assumption that we focus on the strength of our unique identities. This can be of essence in the creation of unity of purpose by tapping into each other's strengths for the welfare of individuals and the state at large.

Language and stylistic aspects of language can be surmised as pointers of a people's aspirations, desires, fears, psychological states and ideologies. A practice of listening to our voices and artistic works can reflect something about our souls in addition to reaffirming our cultural identities. Listening to Kenyan popular music may in a way define our concern in order to learn the psychology of our youth. This would give us an idea of the next world my children (young and still very innocent) are likely to inherit. The soundings of the musical structure in the songs we create and play can thus reveal not just what we are but also the question we are asking, arguably to a society that is in its transient forms, which in addition have formed part of its being and part of the identity of its people.

Towards hypothesis of concealed identities in ethnic patterns of speech

From a loose observation I want to argue that we can learn an aspect of our temperaments from the manner we speak. This can be said to psychologically have an influence on our Identity. From a loose observation I would invite future researchers to interrogate the speech characteristics that are common in Kenya and which in my opinion play a part in defining an aspect of our identity. This can have far reaching effects in building our unity by having a better appreciation of the uniqueness that defines our character in our ethnic diversities.

Kamba language can be said to be musical and romantic upon close examination of its avoidance of consonantal sounds. May be this can tell us something about the Kamba people and their nature. Dholuo can be said to be flamboyant when examined from the way in which the common and ordinary members of the community speak. Kisiis and Merus are purposively forceful languages and arguably this could be a reason why young men from these two communities are arguably short-tempered. Cushitic languages tend to be fast in manner of articulation of words with a lot of staccatos and well intended consonants. This could tell us something about members of these communities. In my view they can be said to be formal and businesslike to mention but a few. These temperament speech identities can be probed further by examining *Information Structure* which is 'the partitioning of sentences into categories such as focus, background, topic, comment' (Büring, 2005: 1). '*Information Structure* doesn't primarily affect the truth conditions of utterances, but more elusive aspects of their meaning,' (Büring, 2005: 2). There is therefore, in the view of this argument an aspect of our identity that has always escaped us which we can trace in the concealed meanings that inform how we speak as a matter of our cultural and ethnic backgrounds.

While intended speech may do much to reveal and at the same time conceal these inner identities, I want to argue that a constant examination of the effect our music, song and dances have on audiences can serve as a window through which we can peer into the private identities of the composers and song writers. Songs in this case can be said to function to reveal an aspect of the artiste's identity.

Music genres in this context can be said to be illocutionary acts, where song, music and dance performances as well as the films we make (about ourselves) become philosophical propositions through which the self is defined. The oral artist should not be studied under a general bracketed group (Kabira, 1983: 1) the same can be said of our music genres. We can, thus, in this case examine the question each genre begs in the manner it tends to construct Kenyan identity. The content and form of the respective music thus becomes a window through which we can peer into conceived identities of selves.

Music forms in this case are 'performative practices' whose content and form function to name and define and therefore give essence to the state of being of the respective practitioners. Consequently, music forms become the mechanism through which different value systems are entrenched and popularized. The processes of composition in this case posit a cultural production process of self definition in addition to giving rise to an artistic work of art.

Cultural interactions have led to importation of music forms that have served to presage new viewership of ourselves from the traditional perspectives other factors such as education, globalization not to withstand. As evidenced in traditional songs, the idea of self was gender oriented where songs functioned to define the roles of individuals in society. This led to the creation of the different genres into which songs were categorized. Upon attainment of independence, Western civilization led to the emergence of new genres of songs such as Rhumba, Funk to mention but too, as a result of emergence of urban centres where the working class in urban centres opted for music that was in English and Kiswahili. Kenyan identities in the old days, I want to argue as evidenced in music that was in our vernacular languages and was ethnic oriented. The songs Kenyans made in this era functioned to define people along ethnic lines. Upon attainment of independence Kiswahili became popular in urban centres and was used as a lingua franca. Musicians in the 60s and 70s as a result, opted to sing their songs in Kiswahili arguably with the aim of reaching a wider audience.

It is wrongly assumed that by singing in Kiswahili the songs of the 60s and 70s functioned to unite Kenyans. I want to take a dissenting position that Kiswahili has functioned to unite Kenyans more than English or our ethnic languages. This position is inspired by the need to call upon each one of us into greater reflections into sincerities within which we use Kiswahili on the assumption that it is a uniting language, yet within us, we remain so divided along ethnic lines. I want to argue that despite providing people of different ethnic backgrounds with a means with which they communicated as they transacted their daily businesses; Kenyans retained their ethnic attitudes and stereotypes as they were before colonization. The fact that Kiswahili was used as a *lingua franca* and in music composition does not necessarily follow that it united Kenyans. What Kiswahili did in this context was to provide the nation with a linguistic hypocritical gown with which Kenyans interacted yet holding on strongly to their ethnic stereotypes. Kiswahili in this context succeeds in concealing the ethnic stereotypes that define the identity of most Kenyans. This is a weak identity that arguably defines an aspect of the true self of most Kenyans but this identity remains concealed. This can be proven if we look at how we tend to coalesce around our ethnic interests when it comes to matters of national interest such as the national elections. Many Kenyans vote along ethnic lines despite having Kiswahili as a national language. I want to argue that assuming Kiswahili unites Kenyans thus far remains a hypothetical position than a reality. What Kiswahili does is to provide Kenyans with a linguistic veil with which they conceal their true selves.

In this context therefore, Kiswahili provide us with a situation of a linguistic contradiction because it is seen on the one hand as if it is uniting Kenyans yet on the other hand it is functioning to sustain their disunity by providing a hypocritical gown with which they hide their true selves from each other. This linguistic practice again becomes a form of an identity of ourselves which again we would not claim. This is an identity which falls within what Derrida terms as an *aporia*. This is a Greek term denoting a logical contradiction. I want to bring out this hypocritical position that exists arguably among many Kenyans that we may garner the courage to address it for better social and national cohesion. This can as a result improve the transparency with which we would claim our Kenyan-hood, identity and belonging. This can be achieved if we weeded out the ethnic bias Kiswahili functions to conceal and in so doing adapt Kiswahili as a language of inclusion and transcending ethnic barriers; but not to use it to hide the hatred we have for others.

We can transcend beyond racial and ethnic stereotypes regardless of the language we use if we cultivate an appreciating attitude of language, colour and beauty of belonging together because we cannot change our ethnicities, neither can we force the other person to change their race or colour. This can be achieved by cultivating a practice of admiring the linguistic apotheosis of the other with a clean slate of sincerity to enjoy the audio poetics in the other person's language and speech patterns. As Michael Jackson puts it in the song 'Heal the World' it starts with the person in the mirror, when we look at ourselves in the mirror. A creation of positive attitude towards each other regardless of our skin and linguistic differences can work towards building a more united Kenya whose value system encompasses identity and belonging.

Identity as a concept begs the question of what is in our minds, about ourselves and about others. Kenyan-hood, identity and belonging begin with the individual practice of telling members of every race, tribe, or creed good things which make them dear to oneself. This boosts the sense of belonging, sense of inclusion and accommodation in every one hence building a greater identity that would qualify for the term 'Kenyan-hood'.

This has been witnessed in today's popular music where young Kenyans appreciate music of the local industry regardless of the language in which the artiste is singing. The artiste in this context will accommodate everyone during the performance regardless of their ethnic background. The fans on the other hand will define a sense of ownership of the music and the artiste regardless of his or her race, class, religion or tribe. Kenyan Hip hop has metamorphosed into different music genres such as Kapuka, Gipuka, Genge, Benga to mention but a few. The questions this paper interrogates are: what aspects of Kenyan identity do these music genres embody? How do they function as pragmatic shifts in our conceived identities? And what aspects of our identity can we deduce from the current music genres?

I want to argue that the current music genres function to integrate our identity and sense of belonging beyond the ethnic stereotypes. This is because current music genres define their audiences outside the ethnic background of the artistes. Music genres such as Ohangla and Mugithi attract not only members of the Luo and Gikuyu respectively for instance, because of the language in which the songs are rendered, but they attract audiences who do not even understand the language. Other music genres such as Genge and Kapuka appear to define Kenyan identity along age and not necessarily ethnic lines. This is because they appear to be favourites of the youths regardless of their cultural background. Popular music in this case appears to define discourses of social cultural integration and homogeneity which if well tapped and harnessed can function to create greater sincerities with which we define our identities not necessarily using Kiswahili but by appropriation of all languages as tools for building greater national unity.

Music as metaphor in this context functions to institute procedures which we appropriate in the quest to define our identity. Metaphor is not in language at all, but in the way we conceptualize one mental domain in terms of another (Lakoff, 1992:185). In this context the concept of metaphor involves an examination of mapping where 'the word *metaphor* has come to mean *a cross-domain mapping in the conceptual system*', metaphor is thought, not language…metaphor is a major and indispensable part of our ordinary, conventional way of conceptualizing the world, (Lakoff, 1992:186). The concept of metaphor in this case becomes a process of mapping practices of being. I want to argue that music practices in this context function to draw aspects of our identity. We can therefore examine aspects of our identity that appear to emerge from current music forms. This can be examined by analyzing the song's lyrics and music structure as mental images where the message and manner of rendition becomes an epitome of self constitution.

At this point, therefore, I want to observe that present music forms that inform and institute a social reordering process where artistes have transcended cultural ethnic milieus in their propagation of Kenyan-hood and self-hood. This is because the current popular music artistes address social issues that members of different cultural backgrounds can identify with. In so doing, the artistes define aspects of identity and belonging along socio-cultural spaces. This consequently, ties our human sensibilities of identity and belonging along our nature as social members of the same society. Music in this context functions to unite us and thus serve to create an identity of ourselves that is more responsive to our need for social belonging.

Form and content that define our music today can be surmised as pointers of a people's aspirations, desires, fears, psychological states and ideologies. A practice of listening to our voices in artistic works can reflect something about our souls in addition to reaffirming our cultural identities. Sound appropriation in music genres can therefore say much about us and consequently function to define an aspect of our identity. A refocusing of our voice(s) towards our inner selves may reveal something about us which we never knew and may be it would reveal something about us that we need to work on in order to improve the influence we have on the world around us. Music in this case reveals much more than the composers intentions.

I, therefore, argue that Kenyan identity can be sought in contexts of multiplicities that exist in transient states as evidenced in our popular music genres. This is evidenced in the audio aesthetic structures that are characteristic of how we compose our music. Current music genres can be said to define attributes of transience where the structural frames of our music reveal a state of a being that is in constant search for its greater essence. Our identity in this case is constituted along temporal states.

A close listening to the music we consume in this context, says something about our psychology as a nation and as individuals. This in addition can give us ideas of the next generation. The soundings of the musical structure in the songs we create and play thus reveal not what we just are but also the question we are asking, arguably of ourselves, our identity and our society. I am called to mind about the aspects of our identity as revealed in the language that defines our creative works of art. This is because as Weedon observes, 'Crucial to theorizing subjectivity and identity is the question of language (12)' our music propagates and popularizes speech practices that serve to define who we are. The urban popular music especially whose main language of mediation is sheng should provoke us to examine the nature of ourselves that this music posits. Owing to the very unstable nature of sheng as a pidgin one can then argue that our urban music reveals a society that is wallowing in its own dilemma. As one Allan Aaron a gospel artiste once told me, as a messenger of God, he sings in sheng because it is the language those he has been sent to preach to, speak. The instabilities and unpredictability and the unstable state of sheng in this case serves to define an aspect of our identity along postmodernism and postmodern discourses. Unlike in the past the music genres in this context presage discourses of self examination and self contestations at the same time. Our identity in this case becomes a process not an end in itself.

The loud heavy kick drum that is common in almost all Kenyan Music genres with the exception of Taraab can, for instance, be said to signify the urgency with which we tend to define ourselves along pressures and do or die aspects of a capitalist state. The loudness that define the sound of our music as semantic texts in this case posits to show that today our ideologies and sense of belonging are marked by a subsumed sense of contestation of how we have been made to think of ourselves. This is because the loudness can be examined as a mapping of self along self interrogative discourses. This can be said to be a reaction to effects of colonial vestiges which we happen to act against in our quest to define our identities and belonging. This in retrospect has functioned to define our identities along traits of aggression as the nature of our being struggles to come to terms with itself.

One can argue that the nature of our music in this context identifies with the complexity of art and artistic texts and their ability or power to articulate the embodiments of humanity in a *language of art* which embody the melodic structures of our music. The natures of our being that remain subsumed and in most cases unspoken about but which are revealed in the artistic forms of our music exist not only to articulate the message inherent in the lyrics but in additional functions to construct aspects of our being and identity. I want to argue that the process of listening to the songs we create in some sort of newness can help trace the various shades of our identities that happen to escape our attention mostly as a result of an inability to think of manifestation of ourselves in our music, poetry, performances and narratives. We can therefore listen to the works of art we create with an aim to see what they reveal of ourselves, our ideologies, identities and sense of belonging.

Works of art in this context are emblems of the society that is responsible for their creation. We can therefore examine an aspect of the selves in us which is reflected in the artistic works we create or consume. This is of essence in policy making and in moral stock taking of ourselves, if we were to remain relevant as stakeholders in the shaping of our future generations. All artistic works are metaphors, saying something, about something else. I guess however, the metaphor is in the philosophical spirit that informs the voice in the song, in the spoken word, in the performed arts, which defines who we are and that haunts how we think of ourselves.

Writers and music artistes in this case create their work bearing in mind, the possible effects their works are to have on members of the society. In this regard, they create their works of art, with a serious focus on sensitivity of the impact their style of writing or singing is to have on their readers, about themselves and the world around them, for writing and song writing and composition are not about the work, but about human life and human values. The literary text or the song in this case is a messenger. A skillful artiste or writer must therefore care about how they deliver the message, most often than not, one may think they are caring while in real sense they are but in the process of further explorations of our identity. Speech techniques and authorial voice in this case remain subsumed in the text. The problem has however remained how to read the written text with the ears in addition to reading it with the eyes. On the part of music, the problem that will remain, therefore, is one of tracing our selves in our music, by examining not what we listen to in a song but by listening to how we listen to the song. Every act of listening in this case defines gaps in its operation of purported choices which we put into practice in how we will tend to listen and interpret the nature of our identity that any song may imply.

Conclusion

How often do we remember when we dress in woollen clothes that it was once a covering of a sheep that was once grazing in some green fields, when we dress in silk do we take time to recall, it was once a worm? And when you dress in cotton would it help just to imagine it was once a plant growing innocently in a cotton field. The same can be said of our arts and their histories. With every song we compose, we are writing our philosophies of culture, poetry and identity as documentations of aspects of ourselves and our being. I think we would then need to care about what we write and how we shall be read in future as Histories. We shall not be there to respond to the accusations that tomorrow's generations will level against us, but it would be a moment of honour if we shall be remembered in praise songs because we left behind a myriad solutions to problems that would mark the challenges of their times in the practices that define the acumen of our music composition and creative writing.

Works cited

Austin, John. *How to do things with words* University Press, Oxford 1975.

Büring, Daniel. *Semantics, Intonation and Information Structure*. University of California Los Angeles (UCLA) 2005.

Fearon, James. *What Is Identity (As We Now Use the Word)?* Stanford, Department of Political Science Stanford University, 1999.

Lakoff, George. The Contemporary Theory of Metaphor, 1992. In Ortony, Andrew (ed.) *Metaphor and Thought* (2nd edition), Cambridge University Press.

Lakoff, George. 'Conceptual metaphor, the contemporary theory of metaphor'. *Cognitive Linguistics: Basic* Readings Ed. Dirk Geeraerts. Berlin New York, Mouton de Gruyter, 2006.

Kabira, Wanjiku. *The oral artist*. Nairobi: East African Education Publishers, 1983.

Kabira, Wanjiku and Karega Mutahi. *Gikuyu Oral Literature*. Nairobi: East African education Publishers, 1993.

Mungai, Mbugua wa. 'Made in Riverwood': (dis)locating identities and power through Kenyan pop music,' *Journal of African cultural studies*: 20:1, 2008: (57-70). Print.

Oishi, Etsuko. *Austin's Speech Act Theory and the Speech Situation*. Esercizi Filosofici, 2006.

Sadock, Jerrold M. *Toward a Linguistic Theory of Speech Acts*. New York: Academic Press. 1974.

Weedon, Chris. *Identity and Culture: Narratives of Difference and Belonging*. McGraw-Hill House: Open University Press, 2004.

9.

Identity and musical score in Tosh Gitonga's 'Nairobi Half Life'

Simon Peter Otieno

Introduction

Kenya has a relatively active film industry that is mapped in varied contexts ranging from independent filmmakers with high-budget practice to indie-film makers working on shoe-string budgets. Some of the practitioners are defined by organizations for instance the Riverwood Ensemble, which is largely populated by filmmakers who operate within the confines of River Road in Nairobi. There is also the Association of Film Producing Educational Institutions of Kenya (AFPEIK), which is a union of educational institutions that participate in an annual film festival that has many films written, directed and shot by students. The television industry houses many filmmakers who eke out a living by producing dramas and local soap operas. In the varied contexts, the character of Kenyan film has generally been marked by challenges of financing, scripting, sound capture, musical scores, acting and lack of strong government support among other aspects. This paper draws attention to, especially, the use of music as a narratological device and marker of identity with close reference to Nairobi Half Life by Tosh Gitonga. The film attracted interest in this research because it is the first film in Kenya to be submitted for the Best Foreign Language Oscar at the eighty fifth Academy Awards and therefore is more likely to have adhered to professional use of musical scoring at international standards. In 2014 the film had many awards at the Africa Magic Viewers Choice Awards. These awards demonstrate that Kenyan film is gaining confidence in parading itself alongside the practice in established global contexts and applying codes comprehensibly for that viewership. It is in the interest of this paper to examine the use of musical scores in Nairobi Half

Life as an entry point into discussing the practice in Kenyan films in order to understand the domestication of this genre.

Methodology

I use the cultural narratology to study how Nairobi Half Life uses musical score. The film creatively uses the score by Xaver von Traver in the narration of the journey by Mwas from the rural context to the 'wild city'. We shall identify the different channels and sources of information in order to assess their individual contribution to, and function in, the filmic composition as a whole with musical score as our main focus in *Nairobi Half Life*. This paper will assess the model against the modeled in its narratological pursuit for as Gerald Prince states in his essay titled 'Surveying Narratology':

> Theory must engage reality; the description must meet the phenomenon; the model must correspond to the modeled. The elaboration of an explicit, complete, and empirically grounded model of narrative accounting for narrative competence... ultimately constitutes the most significant narratological endeavor.

The model will therefore be the yardstick for examining the modeled. Film as a cultural product must exhibit its original context even as it reaches out to the 'outer worlds' within the mode of the model Prince states. It is important to study the musical score in *Nairobi Half Life* because it not only sets the stage for 'world standard' practice of musical scoring but is also a reflection of the application of music in Kenyan film practice as a device for identity in narratological accomplishment. Musical score in film plays a very important role. Some renowned film directors have been quoted to emphasize this role:

Academy Award winning writer-director George Lucas (*Star Wars, American Graffiti*) once told a reporter…"Sound is 50 percent of the movie going experience." But in a recent video interview, *Trance* director Danny Boyle says that sound makes an even greater impact. "The truth is, for me, it's obvious that 70, 80 percent of a movie is sound," he says. "You don't realize it because you can't see it."

Mark Alleyne notes that the academic analysis of the role of sound in cinema has traditionally been marginal at best in film scholarship and yet it is indispensable to the process. The said role justifies a look at *Nairobi Half Life* in the Kenyan context to invite debate into the subject and draw attention to the domestication of musical score in our context. Background or non-diegetical score is sometimes not noticeable because it supplements the action in a feature film and rarely fights for space and attention with the picture. Though rather 'mild' in its role in the film, musical score or even sound tracks bring 'colour' and taste to the picture by emphasizing the mood, intensifying the action or even heightening the perceived tension as the setting and action demand. Roy Prendergast in his text titled *Film Music: A Neglected Art* notes that there is variety of ways of achieving an atmosphere of time and place, or, musically speaking, 'colour'. He adds that despite viewers and many scholars not being keen on the role of music in film:

> In a broad sense, musical color may be taken to represent the exotic or sensuous aspects of music, as distinct from musical structure, or line, which might be considered the intellectual side…Film music is overwhelmingly coloristic in its intention and effect. This is always true when a composer is attempting to create an atmosphere of time and place. Finally, and probably the most important of all, color can be readily understood by a musically unsophisticated film audience.

The musical score renders itself to simple audience who will understand the role it plays depending on their ability to read and understand the intent of the director and/or the musician. Essentially, the source of music should be culturally identifiable or familiar to the viewers for an appreciation of the specific role. *Nairobi Half Life* introduces us to a 'Kenyan' musical idiom when Mwas is in a bus travelling to the city for the first time, which despite being worded in Kikuyu language possesses a rather western texture in instrumentation. It emphasizes the journey of Mwas but just falls short of a clear Kikuyu idiom in its instrumentation texture. Robin Hoffman states that the function of music in the movies is a very wide field and music can serve several purposes that are either important on the emotional side of the movie or enhance the storytelling. Although the music at that point enhances the story, it would be difficult to term as an imprint of a strong identity from the Kikuyu culture upon which the story has been constructed. The cultural idiom becomes imperative as a tool of identity and narratology. It is important to emphasize that African films will have an African score that fully defines the cultural milieu of the setting. Walt Disney's *Lion King* for instance, the story of an African lion family, opens with an African song (although accenting specifically South African music idiom), which already establishes the context of the narratology. To achieve the authentic African identity the film's score was composed by *Hans Zimmer*, who was hired based on his work in two films in African settings, *The Power Of One* and *A World Apart* and supplemented the score with traditional African music and choir elements arranged by Lebo M Zimmer's partners Mark Mancina and Jay Rifkin who helped with arrangements and song production.

In establishing the context through music we derive meaning in the purpose or objective of the score in the ultimate communication intended by the film. *Nairobi Half Life* imitates the Hollywood idiom in many instances in the film but more so within the urban context where the music takes on the hip-hop rap texture. Viewed as the world-standard, Hollywood trends hip-hop and rap to symbolize gangsters in Hollywood films and mark out action in the black American context. Nairobi Half Life carefully obeys the idiom in mapping out the gang of Mwas and Oti as they go out to steal, rob and kill. The plot develops to a climax as Mwas and his gang graduate from stealing lamps and mirrors to robbing state of the art cars. This would necessitate a gradual elevation of the music to depict the change and heightening of the tension and suspense. The musical score comes in handy in the fistfight at Grogon garage that prompts the special branch of the police to pick the gang of Mwas for their ultimate end. We also feel the tension enhanced by the music when Mwas is the sole survivor of a massacre by the police as he runs to Phoenix theatre to play his role in the premier of the play he had been auditioned for and cast. That *Nairobi Half Life* imbibes the Hollywood idiom in musical score may be expected for two reasons. For one, the target audience was well beyond the Kenyan or African audience and secondly the ability of Hollywood to influence world cinemas is unparalleled. It has been noted that:

> Behind this enormous expansion of the concept of classical cinema lies the idea that Hollywood filmmaking has dominated our conception of what a "normal" movie is since the formation of the film studio apparatus between, roughly 1910 and the early 1920s. Thus the U.S. film industry can be treated not only as the most powerful economic force among national cinemas, but relatedly as the most influential model of filmmaking practice in history. The claim is that there are certain identifiable parameters of form and style which have for most of film history served as norms and limitations throughout the world, and these norms are associated most closely with the kinds of films produced most successfully and extensively in the American narrative film industry.

This influence on *Nairobi HalfLife* should therefore not be viewed as a weakness but as an attempt to comply with the 'world standard' for intelligibility with a wider global context. However it is important to analyze how the film domesticates the Hollywood practice to tell a Kenyan story. The paper starts with a general analysis of the story as told by the film composition device and then proceeds to assess the role of the music in the same drawing examples from other films in Kenya and Africa at large.

The story

Nairobi Half Life is about a young man in the village of Murang'a with ambitions of becoming a movie star but who is conned into travelling to Nairobi city with the hope of joining a theatre troupe at the Kenya National Theatre only to end up embroiled in crime. The title already establishes that Nairobi is the destination of the plot. Representative of a section of inhabitants of the city who live 'the half-life', Mwas comes from the rural areas to chase his dream of being a movie star. Quite unexpectedly Mwas ends up in the deadly cycle of crime that engulfs youths who are lured into the attractive city with the promise of money and fame only to end up as the source of a crime, which they must partake in or starve. The journey is as eventful as its narration. Wolf Schmid notes of the eventfulness of action in narratology that:

> ...eventfulness increases in proportion to the extent to which a change of state

deviates from the doxa of the narrative (i.e. what is generally expected in the narrative world)...the essence of the event lies in the fact that it breaks with expectations. A highly eventful change is para-doxical in the literal sense of the word: it is not what we expect. "Doxa" refers to the narrative world and its protagonists and is not equivalent to the reader's script (what the reader expects in the action on the basis of certain patterns in literature or the real world).

On his first day in the city, Mwas is mugged and loses everything (including an expensive radio his uncle sent him to deliver to an Asian friend), ending up in one of the dreaded police cells in the city. The cell is full of people who view their illegal detention and the inhumane conditions in which they are held as normal. Furthermore Mwas ends being assigned to clean the dirty toilet with human waste all over the place. He falls as he washes the place and again cheats our expectation as he tries to accept his condition by singing as he mops the muck. This surprises everyone including the inmates who come to see 'the singer' in the dirty toilet. The fate of Mwas is sealed in this incident. He has ended up in muck and the best he can do is try to make the best of his condition. In the filthy cells, he meets Oti, a petty criminal in the city, who introduces him to his new world. He is alone and has lost his uncle's radio. The only work available is washing dishes in a small dinghy eating joint in a slum. He is soon embroiled in a world of crime where to eat well and enjoy the goodies of the city that is meat, beer and women, he has to steal car parts from parked vehicles in the city.

Despite this mode of survival, Mwas does not give up his ambition to be an actor. He attends an audition at the Phoenix theatre and gets a role in a play. The play is about robbers who break into a rich couple's house, not to steal, but to remind them of the existence of the poor. It replicates accurately the life Mwas is living in reality. As he graduates into stealing cars, Mwas gets embroiled into a clandestine relationship with the special branch of the police where they rob and 'pay tax' to the officers. When the officers realize they are in danger of being exposed they decide to eliminate the entire gang of Mwas. He luckily escapes the murder in which all his friends are killed to go and catch up with the premier performance of the play in which he was cast at the Phoenix theatre.

When the film begins Mwas is selling music and film in CDs and DVDs and is excited to tell the story of the most exciting film in his stock to his prospective clients. He is speaking in Kikuyu language, which perfectly places the action well into the context. It is at this point that he hears about a theatre troupe, 'The Vultures' that is performing in his village shopping centre. He goes to the venue of performance and even interrupts the performance at one point 'stealing' the attention of the audience away from the performers when they take a break. The cue of the music at this point does not in any way reflect the setting of the story, which is a shopping centre in Murang'a County. In terms of identity and the cultural set up the musical cue does not reflect or even hint at the setting. The dominant culture in Muranga is Kikuyu culture and hence the idiom of the music would be expected to reflect the same. Kikuyu culture has rich music, which would have not only defined and invited the viewer into the context but also allowed appreciation of its appeal. The context of the performance of 'The Vultures' troupe allows little room for contextualized music. The implication here is that the shopping centre is 'semi-urban' and so 'The Vultures' perform in Swahili, the urban language in Kenya. The performance is structured like theatre for development (TfD) that is supposed to sensitize the public about corruption among the political elite but which doesn't quite necessarily fulfill the tenets of TfD. This troupe does not have any songs to invite the target audience into the performance as is usually the case with theatre troupes in Kenya. In essence the theatre performance has been used to conveniently propel our protagonist, Mwas, into the world of his dreams and ambitions without seriously addressing its nature and presentation. In community theatre or theatre for development (as the one presented by 'The Vultures') music is important in motivating the participants (both actors and 'spect-actors') into the engagement of the theme. Michela E Vershbow observes correctly that:

> Music does not create political change as a solitary force…rather, it is a conduit for change that stirs a community into action, expresses and calls attention to oppression, and bridges the divide between people of different cultures.

In the performance of 'The Vultures', little or no emphasis was laid in the said use of music. This leaves the story bare. The musical score in *Nairobi Half Life* is not as ambitious as the story.

The diegetic song by Mwas' drunken father, sung in Kikuyu language sets the identity of the context with emphatic clarity. The shock in his mother when he reveals the decision he has made to travel to the city is, however, bare. When Mwas sets out the following morning, there is no accompanying music, which misses the emotion of 'leaving home'. Many people have left their rural homes to come to the city and this is many a time not an easy decision for any family. The score could easily have captured this based on the cultural context. The non-diegetic score catches up with the story when the bus ferrying Mwas is almost at the city. The sound track is in Kikuyu language but the instrumentation cannot be related to the culture. Graeme Harper asks very interesting questions in terms of using music in film whether particular national media have culturally identifiable styles – say the cinemas of India, or whether the films of particular countries in a continent such as Europe, or in certain portions of a national population, such as those of the African-American population within the context of American cinema generally have an identity. He further muses whether particular periods suggest different things in the evolution of the sound track and finally asks what the role of the listener is in all these. It would be a mouthful to answer Harper in this paper but the point is made. The taste of the audience is paramount and that builds on an identifiable or familiar musicality. Identity in film defines its geographical and cultural source and despite the fact that *Nairobi Half Life* defies our parochial domain heading onto the global platform, it urgently needed to reach that pedestal with a Kenyan/Kikuyu/Nairobian 'rubberstamp'. Harper states of this identity in the music that it is in terms of a culture or cultural conditional system of cultural signs that are incorporated into the sound or, indeed, the music – that itself is often considerably culturally charged, often so much so that audiences can determine even the minor influence of particular local or distant styles. Particular film periods, film styles or even directors with the use of particular musical genre can be helpful in better recognizing a component of audience taste and response. Graeme notes that:

> These questions come with historical as well as textual relevance. They relate likewise to notions of the *use* of sound and music: for example, they relate to questions of politics in the choice and positioning of music; or to questions of cultural hegemony in the favouring of a particular sound or set of sounds, or in the manipulation of the relationship between sound and image.

Language can have a metaphoric tint. So it is with the language of sound in film exhibited in *Nairobi Half Life*. We rarely pay attention to the sound of the music until one asks questions about it. This is perhaps so because of the skillful nature of the score composition and the intelligent placement of the same on the timeline.

When Mwas is in River Road the musical cue adopts Kenyan hip-hop, which effectively gives the gangster feel. The hip-hop reveals the rebellion in the gang that Mwas joins justifying their action in the Sheng' words translated as 'I have arrived in the city and I am looking for work and money'. The song reveals a capitalistic quest that places the action of the gang after they have stolen and sold car headlamps and side mirrors to a 'client'. The 'social gap' between the rich and the poor is the implied pointer to the gang's action. This is further revealed in the play that Mwas is rehearsing at Phoenix Theatre; about 'robbers' who break into a wealthy neighborhood just to remind the rich couple that they (the poor) exist. The story of the musical cue effectively begins here. The contextual musical 'story' ends after the hip-hop as the film gets into Hollywood 'mood creation' mode of musicality; which works in many respects for the fast paced ending.

Whereas it is impossible to debate the actual composition that the score composer ought to explore, Harper notes that inevitably, the decisions that are made about how sound should sound are based on subjective technical perspectives which in turn help shape what the public perceives as accurate sound reproduction. At the end of the film we encounter a sound track in Swahili language, which was first featured when Mwas was in the slum. With a texture of music from the coastal culture the question that is raised concerns what is 'Swahili' in the context and the action. This presents a problem as the hip-hop used already calls home the urban context with its mix of cultures. Eddie Kalish notes that the majority of the background music albums come off only to the point of establishing a main theme. He notes that the rest of the disks are usually an assortment of fragments, which don't mean much musically or commercially in many films. F H Richardson in his essay titled, 'Plain Talk to Theater Managers and Operators: Seating/Music,' acknowledges that music is a matter of greater importance than many moving pictures than theatre managers seem to imagine. Hugo Riesenfeld in the essay, 'Music and Motion Pictures,' notes that music in film ought to be controlled by the popular music of the day that may be changed in film according to the taste of the viewers. Although *Nairobi Half Life* may not be entirely guilty of 'cultural-neglect' in part, the emphasis of identity is a subject that needs to be taken seriously if Kenyan films are to make it to the world stage and demand their rightful place.

Conclusion

It is only fair to take note that professional score composers are lacking in Kenya, while hiring one from outside the country would be very expensive. This may explain the reason for the Kenyan film directors hiring the services of Xaver Von Traver. Although this may partly explain the gaps in identity, it is noticeable that this is a consistent practice in Kenyan films. *Malooned* by Bob Nyanja is another 'world standard' film featuring two characters, a Luo man and a Kikuyu woman, locked in a toilet for a long weekend. The musical score is not used to identify the two communities. The director, Bob Nyanja, explains that he considered the two characters as urbanites and did not see the need for a score that would delve into their cultural identities. This has also been observed in the television serials. The serial *Papa Shirandula* presents a Luhya man who has come to the city as a security officer. The score of the serial has no identity of Papa Shirandula and his roots. The serial titled *Inspector Mwala* also purports to present a Kamba policeman who rises to the rank of inspector but again the score demonstrates nothing of Kamba culture. It may not just be a culture of ignoring musicians. This demonstrates a lack of professional score composers in the country who understand the nuances of film and visual media. We could perhaps begin with the practice as Erno Rapee notes in the essay 'Selections from Encyclopedia of Music for Pictures'.

> A great deal has been written on how to arrange music to feature pictures. Experience and observation have taught me that the simplest procedure is as follows: firstly, determine the geographic and national atmosphere of your picture; secondly, embody every one of your important characters with a theme.

This experience could be an excellent starting point for our good musicians interested in choosing a career in score compositions. An emphatic example is evident in a number of South African films. Although, among others, films like *Cry Freedom, Yesterday* and *Cry the Beloved Country* all exhibit well thought out scores, *Sarafina* stands out as a film with a score that was carefully tailor-made to suit its thematic engagement. The musical cues fall into place in the narrative like a jigsaw puzzle. With a drive towards the freedom of Nelson Mandela, it exploits the South African musical idiom for the struggle against apartheid. Michela E Vershbow in 'The Sounds of Resistance: The Role of Music in South Africa's Anti-Apartheid Movement' observes about music in film that it would be better seen as an attempt to allow the viewer to hear and see (and perhaps feel) the power of music in forging political change, resisting oppression, strengthening community, and uniting people of different race and status. *Nairobi Half Life* may only boast of the hip hop as the music that was composed with the screen play in mind. In this way, the opportunity to link the viewer with the specific cultural setting is missed for as Schulkin notes; music and song are conduits for forging links across barriers, for making contact with others, and for being indoctrinated with the social milieu. Prendergast also states that 'musical color' in a film can be achieved through the use of musical material indigenous to the locale of the film. This is the most emphatic signature for engraving the contextual identity of a film. Sometimes it may be a shared already known musical cue like the ones in *Sarafina* or the use of a musical idiom of a people through the use of a musical instrument and/or the linguistic parole of the context like Ayub Ogada practices. Ogada's *Koth Biro* is not a traditional song among the Luo. No one in Luo land had ever heard of that song before but then how do we identify it with Luo culture? Apart from the language of the song, which is Luo, he uses the famous *orutu*; a renowned Luo musical instrument. The composition is hence 'fresh' but with an unmistakable identity. It has been used in several international films including the science-fiction *At the Gates* to give the production a feel of an African context for a western audience. The practice of film scoring can be learned but also demands a lot of intuition and a deep understanding of the people's love of music. It is a practice that demands both practical experience as well as learned observation/ listening to perfect the art of making the viewer to 'see the sound and hear the picture'.

Works Cited

Attenborough, Richard [dir] *Cry Freedom* 1987.
Citizen TV Production *Papa Shirandula*, 2016.
Citizen TV Production *Inspekta Mwala*, 2016.
Chris Menges(dir), *A World Apart* [DVD], 1988.
Harper, Graeme (ed.) *Sound and Music in Film and Visual Media*. Bloomsbury Publishing Inc., London: 2009.
John G Avildsen(dir), *The Power of One* [DVD], 1992.
Julie Hubbert (Ed.) *Celluloid Symphonies: Texts and Contexts in Film Music History*. University of California Press, London: 2011.
Kindt, Tom and Hans-Harald Müller (Eds) *What is Narratology?* Walter De Gruyter, New York: 2013.

Mark Alleyne *Sounds Reel: Tracking the Cultural History of Film Sound Technology*
Bloomsbury Academic, an imprint of Bloomsbury Publishing, London: 2009.
Michela E Vershbow*The Sounds of Resistance: The Role of Music in South Africa's*
Anti-Apartheid Movement [http://www.studentpulse.com [accessed 12th March 2016].
Rob Minkoff, Roger Allers (dirs), *Lion King* [DVD], 1994.
Robin Hoffman <http://www.robin-hoffmann.com>[accessed 17 March 2016].
Roodt, Darrel [dir] *Cry the Beloved Country* 1995.
— [dir], *Sarafina* [DVD], 1994.
— [dir] *Yesterday* 2004.
Rosen,Phillip *Narrative Apparatus, Ideology, A Film Theory Reader*. New York,
Columbia University Press. 1986. *SemioticBasics* <http://faculty.washington.edu>[accessed 14 May 2016].
Roy M Prendergast (1992) *Film Music: A Neglected Art* London: W W Norton and Company.
Schulkin, Jay and Greta B Raglan *The Evolution Of Music And Human Social Capability* [http://journal.
frontiersin.org] [accessed 2 May 2016].
Tosh, David Gitonga (dir), *Nairobi Half Life* 2012.
'Trance' dir Danny Boyle: Sound is up to 80% of a Movie [http://blog.dolby.com] [accessed 12 March 2016].
Vershbow, Michela E *The Sounds of Resistance: The Role of Music in South Africa's Anti-Apartheid Movement* [http://www.studentpulse.com] [accessed 3 May 2016].

10.

The forgotten citizens: A search for identity and belonging for women religious

Jane Nambiri Ouma

Abstract

Ngcobo, Laureta (1986) in her essay, African Motherhood, Myth and Reality,' offers the African traditional and cultural definition of a woman as, a wife, mother and grandmother. This definition appears to exclude women religious, who are sisters living in convents, but whom even the various women forums working for the space of women and women emancipation such as Maendeleo ya Wanawake (MYWK), Federation of Women Lawyers in Kenya (FIDA) and many others, appear not to recognize, thus, raising the question of identity and belonging for this group of women, in what one may want to call the normal, or shall we call it ordinary, world of women.

This paper attempts to enter the world of these religious women who confide that even their very ancestral families operate as if they (sisters) never existed or no longer exist as part of the family. In trying to understand what these religious women feel about, and how they attempt to negotiate the spaces of social and cultural identity, and/or familial and civil belonging, I took time to collect personal narratives from different religious sisters, upon which the discourses of this paper are based. The paper is premised on the view that oral testimonies offer an invaluable source of information on a society and that the collective autobiographies of a people can be translated into the biography of their nation or profession, (Muchiri, 2014).

Key: Forgotten women, Citizens, Narratives, Identity, Belonging, Women Religious.

Introduction

Identity and belonging are key words in a human being's life. This is because identity gives an individual a sense of self and personhood. It is this sense that paves way for one to gain membership to the larger society, thereby giving them the sense of belonging. Samovar, et al (2007), explain identity as the reflective self-image that we each derive from our family, cultural, social, ethnic, political and individual socialization process. The self-image is reflected and expressed in different contexts defining who we think we are, and where we feel we belong. In particular, a person's strongest and most intimate sense of belonging lies in their relationship with their family, their culture, and their social ties, and therein lie their most legitimate identity and surefootedness, Samovar, et al (ibid, 111). Apparently, therefore, identity and belonging go hand in hand, each determining the other and giving one the said sense of self and personhood.

The relationship between a person's identity and belonging, and their family, cultural and social ties is the anchor of this paper as it endeavours to interrogate the sense of identity and belonging for the African Catholic Religious women, commonly known as sisters. The vocation to religious life is abundant. The number of sisters can hardly be quantified. About ninety nine percent of the women religious now in Africa are Africans. In spite of the evident success of missionary work in Africa seen in the teeming population of Catholic sisters who have embraced religious life, there is an evident lack of depth in the understanding and acceptance of who these sisters are, (Kanu, 2012).

The interest in this group of women stems from the fact that they live in convents, in a manner, so to say, enclosed and kind of closed away from the rest of the society and only allowed specific interaction. The question of identity and belonging for this group of women becomes critical for the fact that their vocation demands that they leave their kin and kith, including their cultural practices to go and leave away in the convent which espouses a different culture and doctrine. The question really is: How do they maintain, if not negotiate their familial, cultural, social, or socio-political identity and belonging from which they have apparently been alienated? The question becomes even more crucial given that the women join the new vocation having already developed strong and intimate ties with these institutions of their formative years. Indeed, while many of them join after their high school – at age 18 and above – some even join after college.

This paper tries to understand what these religious women feel about, and how they attempt to negotiate the spaces of social and cultural identity, and/ or familial and civil belonging. The methodology adopted relates to personal narratives. According to Buchanan (2006), a researcher uses the language of the narrative because in the words of Susan Shaw:

> Narrative gives shape to experience and turns the raw data of experience into

meaning. Therefore, narrative represents a primary or privileged form of discourse and significant way of knowing. Narrative also offers possibilities of legitimating notions of reality or destabilizing them. These self-narratives are shaped within meta-narratives, or larger stories…

This research takes personal narratives of religious sisters in Africa and treats them as autobiographical encounters by which the sisters tell, not just their stories but the stories of our own lives as well, (Bruner, 2004, p. 694). The narratives bring out life in stories and as stories, Buchanan (2006). Using the Feminist lens the paper captures life that is hardly documented if not forgotten. The discourses of the paper are specifically based on the analysis of personal narratives from twelve religious sisters, from eight different congregations, whom we interviewed. The interview sessions were held at the participants' convenient places, sometimes in their offices or community space. The sampling technique employed was purposive, whereby participation was restricted to Roman Catholic religious sisters in Africa. The participants, (names indicated are not their real names) were rather invited through personal contact. The selection was inclusive of the different categories of sisters who live religious life in terms of temporary and finally professed including leaders such as superiors/ formators. This kind of selection was to ensure that information-rich cases were included, acting as a boost for validity and reliability of the narratives, (Eze, et a, 2015).

The paper is premised on the view that oral testimonies offer an invaluable source of information on a society and that the collective autobiographies of a people can be translated into the biography of their nation or profession, (Muchiri, 2014).

Familial identity and belonging

The family is perhaps the oldest and most fundamental of all human institutions and found in every culture. Comprised of one's kinsfolk, the family greatly influences an individual. Indeed, the intimacy of an individual to his or her kinsfolk cannot be gainsaid. Such intimacy is easily captured in a popular Kiswahili saying from Kenya which says: *Mla nawe hafi nawe ila mzaliwa nawe,* (Friends who dine with you, however close, cannot die with you/for you, except one who is born with you). This saying underscores the ties one has with a blood relative such as a brother or sister. In her testimony, Sister (Sr) Jane Francis, 48, points out, thus:

> It's never the same. It's special. It's different what you feel towards a fellow sister in the convent and what you feel towards your blood sister. When you quarrel with a fellow sister at the convent, you can keep the grudge and keep avoiding her. When it is with your blood sister you'll always be on the lookout for the opportunity to reconcile.

88

Sr Jane Francis then narrated to me her episode when she fell ill:

> After my operation all sisters from our convent came to visit – several times, in
> fact. Some were even from other convents and congregations. It was particularly
> humbling when Mother Superior herself came to see me. But it all appeared as
> routine. They would sit on the chairs in the room and wish me quick recovery. The
> day my mother and younger sister visited, I just knew when I was already on my
> feet hugging them. It was my best day. My mother sat at the side of my bed holding
> my hand and my tears started to flow. I couldn't explain why I was crying as I felt
> no pain. Meanwhile I was dying to have her touch my cheek the way she used to
> do when I was young. The urge overwhelmed me, so I pulled her hand myself and
> placed it on my left cheek. It was the best feeling ever.

One can easily read the sister's emotional feelings when her family visited her
in hospital. Apparently this was a feeling she could not experience even when
Mother Superior, her congregational head visited. It perhaps did not matter that
Sr Jane Francis had twenty-seven years since she left home. Her blood relatives
had that touch on her.

It appears, though, that in spite of the joy family ties would bring them,
majority of the sisters are not accorded the opportunity. As Sr Anne explained,
her family members started seeing her as not being one of them once she joined
the convent. *"I realized that whenever I came to visit, my sisters and brothers
would be ill at ease, refraining from doing certain things in my presence. It
made me feel like an outsider."* This kind of experience appeared common
to most of the sisters we talked to. Indeed as Sr Anne explained, the family
members seemed to demarcate out two worlds; the real and the ideal. They saw
themselves as belonging to the real world – the world of ordinary people – or
to put it better, 'normal' humans with the license to do things that were human,
while I am placed in the ideal world – the supernatural world where they expect
me to be angelic. *"They could even feel scandalized when I do as simple a thing
as to dance to a traditional tune. It makes one feel so plastic. And the fact that
I have to remain in my nun's uniform when I am at home does not help matters.
You always feel different."*

The following excerpt vividly captures the way Sr Anne and perhaps other
sisters see themselves:

> We are normal people, a community of sinners; that said yes to a call from God. We
> come from many different walks of life – we have nurses, social workers, catechists,
> teachers, and administrators. What we have in common is that we have all become
> convinced of the fact that God is calling us to live in a way that is decidedly
> countercultural. We are not holier or better than others. We are ordinary people who
> have their own experiences with the joys and sorrows of life, aspiring to live our
> lives with some purpose. We are still a part of the society and enjoy things that other
> people do: running, hiking, reading and so on.

Considering Sr Anne's narrative, she suffers a clash of identities; the identity she feels she has that should tie her to her people and the one that she carries from the convent, symbolized by her nun's uniform. Apparently, while she feels that she is still one of them, her people see her as the 'other', who quit from their league and whose belonging is not here.

But if Sr Anne's story sounds discriminatory enough, Sr Gabriel's narrative can be equated to an identity and belonging uprooted. According to Sr Gabriel, she had at first been lucky to have a brother who had been a seminarian and who understood the kind of exclusion his sister could suffer. He, therefore, set aside a room which his nun sister would sleep in whenever she visited from the convent. Things went well until her brother passed on. The next time she visited, her room had been rented out to a stranger. When she complained, nobody seemed to listen. Next time she visited again the small house had been pulled down altogether. Since nobody seemed to bother about where she would sleep, including her own mother, she saw that it was clearly being communicated to her that her space here was no longer available. As it was late she slept in her mother's house, but her mother grumbled the whole night to the effect that grown women do not sleep in their mothers' houses. *"Why don't you find a husband to give you shelter?"* her mother finally exploded. *"I've never felt like going home again since that day."* Sr Gabriel concluded.

In the case of Sr Gabriel, it is clear that her family no longer sees her as a member of the family. That a family would try to erase from their midst the identity and belonging of a woman who has joined the convent is a very common practice. Like Sr Gabriel, Sr Letitia also complained that her kin had apparently *'logged her out'*, she said laughing. When her own mother passed on in 2010, nobody bothered to inform or call her in spite of being quite within reach. Apparently one would even ride a bicycle and call her, if they couldn't get her phone number. *"It was as if I didn't exist,"* she now suddenly gets enveloped in intense sadness.

It is evident from some of the stories narrated by the sisters that many of them are struggling against a strong tide to maintain their identity and belonging in their homes of birth. Indeed as some point out, it is hard to let go. This explains the strong bond one has with his or her kin. It is hard to replace this identity, as Sr Anne explained. Apparently, the acquaintances one makes in the convent cannot just suffice. The emotional attachment she has to her mother whom she lived with for only twenty years is far greater than that to her Mother Superior whom she has lived with for the greater part of her adult life. How are the sisters then coping with this loss? The following excerpt from one sister who insisted that her name should not be included, perhaps captures the feelings of some:

> The fact that I have chosen to live as a woman religious costs me deeply even now in my later years as an elderly sister now bedridden... I will leave no children of my own in this world. And yet, to give myself to God and to all his people is what l do want to do with my life...l have been rejected by my own family (brothers, sisters

and parents). What is the gain? Anyway, I cannot turn back. Am losing all for the sake of Christ.

This sounds like one who has despaired. There is nothing else she can do but to hang on. Perhaps if the clock were to be rewound…She keeps on for the sake of Christ.

Cultural identity and belonging

The discussion on culture in this paper is meant to focus on a people's customs, beliefs, values and tested practices, and in particular how these influence the way people view themselves and the world around them. As Samovar, et al (ibid) observes, one's culture supplies one's identity, for what is carried in one's culture is both deeply felt and enduring.

As already observed, the women who join religious life to live in the convent do so when they are adults. This means that by the time they are joining, they are already deeply entrenched in their people, and that their cultural identities and worldview are already formed. It is noteworthy that the convent – a purely Western Christian institution – operates on a culture whose principles are different from those of the African setup in which the women were socialized. This begins to give a hint on the identity crisis that they are likely to encounter. As Sr Theodora explained in her narrative: *"Life at the convent is different. Many of the things I knew and believed while at home are not the things here."* However, to emphasize how sometimes old habits die hard, Sr Theodora confirmed to me that they too live in fear of witchcraft: *"I know of my colleague here who, whenever she visits her family, comes back with charms and stuff for witchcraft."* I then ask: 'Do you fear her?' Sr Theodora then laughs and asks: *"Fear her! Who doesn't fear witchcraft?"*

It interested me to learn that there would be fear of witchcraft in the convent, but then this perhaps goes to confirm how entrenched beliefs can be. It is fear of African witchcraft in a Christian institution. Indeed the sister mentioned to me that her Western colleagues in the convent dismiss this fear as rubbish, for Jesus Christ came to destroy the power of witchcraft. Yet as Sr Theodora quips, it is because they themselves are yet to come face to face with the power of witchcraft. *"It exists, it is real,"* she concludes.

If Sr Theodora's opinion on witchcraft may not be important, it reveals the dual identity that she faces. Having perhaps grown up in a culture that believed the existence and power of witchcraft, this fear would follow her into the convent and her very closeness to Jesus Christ does not seem to alleviate this fear. It is, therefore, logical to assign her two identities as far as this belief is concerned: the physical identity living in the convent and the mental identity still stuck with her family that lives in perpetual fear of witchcraft.

Incidentally, while the sisters find themselves at a crossroads in certain matters of belief and principle, the kind of identity society may assign them as women is most interesting. Ngcobo, Laureta (1986) in her essay, 'African Motherhood, Myth and Reality', offers the African traditional and cultural definition of a woman as, a wife, mother and grandmother. This definition appears to exclude these women religious. Culturally, they apparently do not qualify as women: they don't get married, so they cannot be wives; they live celibate lives, so cannot become mothers; and they can't be mothers, so they cannot become grandmothers. Who are they then?

The value attached to wifehood and motherhood in the African setup cannot be gainsaid. Motherhood, so to say, forms the common denominator in debates defining a woman, (Wangari Waweru, 2013). Similarly, Muthoni, 1994, observes that girl children in the African society are from their earliest stage of their life predestined to look forward to marriage, wifehood and motherhood. If what Muthoni (ibid) points out is anything to go by, then the girl who joins the convent instead of going to get married, fails the societal test and could even be considered a rebel and an outcast. This perhaps partly explains the kinds of treatment that the sisters mentioned in the previous section were being subjected to.

That a woman must get married and have children is an expectation that even very young children have been trained to have. Sr Lucy, narrated to me that every time she visited her sister, now late, her children would ask why she doesn't bring her own children so that they could play with them? The elder daughter, about eight, would ask where I leave my husband. *"This was in spite of being in my nun's uniform. When I told her that I was not married, the girl would shout 'you are lying' and would run off. The girl would next time again come to ask about my husband. I realized that she already had the notion that a woman must have a husband."*

Sr Lucy relates with amusement how her sister – perhaps immersed in the very view that a woman should be married – tried to trick her:

> When one time I visited her, she invited a certain gentleman to the house and she sneaked out leaving me alone with the man, as if to say: 'if you are unmarried for lack of a man, there is one'. I excused myself and went to sleep leaving the man in the living room. I was to later learn that my mother was happy about what my sister had done. The moment the door was closed having me in a room with a man, I had symbolically got married. My mother was no longer worried about the curse I would have brought to the family due to my unmarried status. I was amused.

While Sr Lucy found this move by her sister amusing, she regrets the distance her sister keeps from her: *"The day she introduced me to her husband, she said: 'This is Sr Lucy.' Then – I imagined – as an afterthought, she added: 'my sister'. I somehow, felt some element of being treated as the 'other'. Apparently, my being Sr Lucy came first instead of my being her sister. It even hurts me that her husband has never addressed me as 'sister-in-law. He always calls me Sr Lucy, I guess having taken queue from my sister. You feel so distanced".*

Socio-economic identity

Muleka, 2007, observes that Abakhayo like majority communities in Africa attach economic value to their girl children. A girl child is hoped to fetch the family wealth through the dowry her husband will pay at marriage. A girl who joins the convent is perhaps seen to subvert or undermine this expectation. She – one would say – serves a subtracting instead of adding role. She is, thus, likely to be resented. Sr Patricia from Uganda, now pursuing her PhD at a university, recalls how her mother reacted when she realized that her daughter was not going to change her mind about joining the convent: *"Why are you doing this to me?"* she asked me with tears in her eyes. *"How have I wronged you to deserve this? Have I been a bad mother to you?"* How did Sr Patricia take this? *"Of course I was shocked, but if I thought this was going to be the biggest shock, I was mistaken. My father's reaction shocked me more. On hearing about my decision, he was silent for some time and when he spoke, he sounded calm but the bitterness in his words was obvious: 'How I regret wasting my money on you! Now is this the way you are paying me back?'"*

Somehow, Sr Patricia's parents' reaction is actually understandable. Their daughter had apparently decided to conspire with 'those white women in the convent' to deny them the cattle and other property that would have come if their daughter were to get married. It didn't help matters that the sisters at the convent who earn a salary from employment surrender their earnings to their community.

Apparently, therefore, a girl who joins the convent betrays the socio-economic identity that the society in general and family in particular has associated her with. She is now seen as a

liability. So the family may decide to strip her of her belonging. She is kind of ostracized and in a manner of speaking becomes a *persona non grata*. This of course must be a regrettable state for those concerned. Indeed, as Sr Lucy (met earlier on) opines: *"Rejection by one's family can be devastating. It kills your personhood. If you survive, you henceforth feel like a tree that has been uprooted."* If anything, this only confirms the premium placed on one's sense of belonging.

The metaphor of 'uprootedness' seems to pervade the life in the convents. This is perhaps why Sr Lucy keeps visiting her people, *"even when I am aware that they detest me. They are my actual family, and ostracize me as they may, going to them gives me some identity and sense of belonging, however far fetched,"* she asserts.

Social-political identity

It is common knowledge that social- political organizations such as *Maendeleo ya Wanawake (an organization for the development of women),* Federation of Women Lawyers in Kenya (FIDA), among other women's groupings do not invite, leave alone consider, the contribution of the women in the convents. On their part, the sisters appear to see these organizations as far removed from their world.

I tried to find out what Sr Imelda knows about Maendeleo ya Wanawake Organization. She responded that she was aware that the organization routed for the emancipation of women. *"Does the organization also represent you people in the convent?"* I asked. *"No, no no no!"* she replied. *"It is a women's organization".* I interpreted this response in two ways: one the organization did not represent the interests of the women in the convents. This interpretation came from Sr Imelda's strong denial with four 'Nos'. No, the organization did not represent the interests of the women in the convents.

Meanwhile, the second part of her answer left something unsaid, which perhaps Sr Imelda was not aware of. Her answer seemed to exclude the convent people from the league of women. *"It is a women's organization".* If it was a women's organization, yet it had nothing to do with the women in the convents, did the organization consider them as part of its fraternity? If so, did it ever seek to include them? On the other hand, did Sr Imelda consider herself to have any kind of stake in such an organization? Otherwise, did this answer have some inkling of self-exclusion? Is it possible that Sr Imelda sometimes sees herself as not belonging to the league of women? Of course this latter question is prompted by her answer: *"It is a woman's organization".*

When all is said and done, the conclusion that comes out is that the socio-political women's organizations such as *Maendeleo ya Wanawake,* have no space for the women religious, who furthermore do not participate in elective political positions in parliament or elsewhere. This means that these groups of women are also missing on the political scene.

Which identity and sense of belonging?

Right from the family level, it appears evident that the women religious residing in convents suffer two types of identities. Identity one is what this paper may call 'uprooted identity' and second is what we may call 'distorted identity'. Uprooted identity applies to those sisters whose families have, so to say, rejected them as happens to Sr Lucy when her family decides to have nothing to do with her. For Sr Lucy, her familial identity and belonging have been destroyed, and perhaps what she can only hold onto is her membership at the convent, which one sister had pointed out, cannot give one a complete sense of identity and belonging as apparently nothing can replace the familial sense of belonging.

Distorted identity leaves one at a crossroads, holding onto one identity while prophesying a different identity. When Sr Theodora, for instance, continues to live in fear of witchcraft – an identity she developed from childhood, but which remains part of her world view, even when she becomes a Christian and a sister in a convent, her definite identity remains blurred. This perhaps explains the difficulty that goes with trying to change identity. As observed earlier, identity is often deep and enduring. The greater difficulty in changing lies in the fact that this identity is rooted in the familial and cultural ties and the attempt to change to the second identity, rather comes late in the day. What we mean here is that the member joins the convent when she is already an adult and when her identity and sense of belonging seem to be already decided, or formed.

The fact of being rendered into uprooted or distorted identities removes the sisters from the mainstream if not conventional identity, which perhaps explains their faded status and the temptation to see them as the forgotten lot. Similarly, left out of most activities at the family and community level, their identity and belonging at national level becomes, so to say, empty and pointless as national consciousness is simply the aggregate of performance at the lower levels.

Conclusion

This paper has attempted to interrogate the identity and belonging for the women religious living in the convents. From the narratives of themselves narrated by the sisters themselves, the paper has found out that majority of the sisters feel that their decision to join the convent diluted their familial, cultural, social-economic and sociopolitical ties, something that has often made them feel uprooted if not possessing distorted identity. This position appears to isolate them from the mainstream identity, a fact that diminishes their participation in the mainstream life, thereby fading their presence in the mainstream discourses. Failing to feature in majority facets of mainstream life, the sisters, kind of remain forgotten every time issues congregate people at the family, community and national levels. Apparently, while events are taking place in the day to day life, the sisters are excluded because the ordinary society – which sees itself as living in the real world, finds no necessity to include the sisters as they are taken to be living in another world, the ideal world, the superhuman world.

References

Baawobr, K R. (2014). *Consecrated Life in Africa: Chances and Challenges.*

Retrieved on 18 July, 2016. From: http://www.africanmission-mafr.org/Baawobr_richard_consecrated_Life_in_Africa_2014. pdf

Bruner, J. (2004). *Actual minds, possible worlds.* Cambridge: MA: Harvard University Press.

Buchanan, R. (2006). *Unveiling Angela Merici: A Pre-Modern Narrative for a Post-Modern World.* Retrieved

on 18 July, 2016. From: http://oldreligiouseducation.net/member/02_papers/buchanan.pdf Eze, C. et al. (2015). *Catholic Religious Sisters' Identity Dilemmas as Committed and Subjugated Workers:*

A Narrative Approach. Retrieved on 1 September 2016. From: http://link.springer. com/article/10.1007/s13644-014-0202-1.

Kanu, I A. (2012). *Inculturation and the Christian faith in Africa.* International Journal of Humanities and Social Science Vol. 2 No. 17; September 2012. Retrieved on 1 September 2016. From: http://www.ijhssnet.com/journals/Vol_2_No_17_September_2012/25.pdf

Muchiri, J. (2014). *'Understanding Modern Korea through Oral Testimonies,'* in Hekima: Journal of the Humanities and Social Sciences. Volv1, Number 1. University of Nairobi.

Muleka, J. (2007). 'Images *of Women in Abakhayo Bweyaq Oral Poetry and their Significance for Girl*

Children.' PhD Thesis, University of Nairobi.

Muthoni, N. (1994). 'Women Giver of Life,' in *Contesting Social Death: Essays on Gender and Culture.* Ngcobo, L. (1986). *'African Motherhood, Myth and Reality',* in Holst Petersen, Kirstein (ed.) Criticism

and Ideology: Second African Writers' Conference Stockholm 1986. Uppsala: Scandinavian of

African Studies, 150.

Samovar, L A. et al. (2007). *Communication between Cultures.* Thompson Wadsworth: USA.

Wakahiu, J. (2015). *Journey of faith: African girls and religious life.* Retrieved on 18 July, 2016. From: *http://globalsistersreport.org/column/trends/journey/journey-faith-african-girls-and-religoius-life-31346.* Waweru, W. (2013). *Postulations on Motherhood in Africa*: A Review of Margaret Ogola's *The River and the Source* and Buchi Emecheta's *The Joys of Motherhood.* M.A. Thesis, University of Nairobi.

11.

The journey to identity, belonging and citizenship of the girl child in the traditional African home

Joseph Muleka

Abstract

Among the Luhya – a populous patriarchal community in Western Kenya – the girl child today, as in the past, is thought of as a temporary member of her ancestral home who on coming of age will get married and leave for her marital home for good. It is, thus, at her marital home that she is supposed to actually belong and, so to say, have permanent citizenship. Perhaps it is, for this reason that she is not allocated property (including land), in her ancestral home. The implication of this omission presumably being that this is to be found in her marital home. The girl child's identity, therefore, as she grows up, is moulded on this premise. Through the community's oral art-forms that she interacts with: narratives, songs, proverbs, jokes and even people's conversations, she is trained to perceive this position – which she does without any questions, for being her people's oral literature, it comes so spontaneously that she perhaps sees it as the most natural thing. Yet as Uwakweh, (1998), observes, girl children in patriarchal African setups often face frustrations which sometimes translate to self defining actions of the young girl and later of the grown-up woman.

This paper analyses some of the Luhya oral poetry touching on women and girl children in an attempt to trace the journey of the girl child to identity, belonging and citizenship, interrogating if there is a relationship between this journey and the frustrations the girl child faces, that Uwakweh refers to above. But even of greater significance, the paper ventures to find out if the girl child achieves this identity and belonging, and the significance of this for her citizenship at the national level.

Key words: Identity, Belonging, Citizenship, Girl child, Patriarchy, African set-up

Introduction

'Literature results from conscious acts of men in society', (Wa Thiong'o, 1978:6). Consequently, literature is a reflection of the wishes of the society that produces it. It forms an integral part of a people's lives, and through it one can see the history, philosophy and perceptions of the said people about situations and about other people – how the said people define the world in relation to themselves, (Muleka, 2009). It is from this premise that this paper attempts to understand the way the Abakhayo community, which is a sub-branch of the Luhya, views the girl child. The paper does this by studying the community's oral poems which touch on girl children. In particular, the paper tries to interrogate the identity and sense of belonging for a girl child as expressed in the oral poetry of a community such as that of Abakhayo, which, being patriarchal in its social set-up tends to favour boys over girls.

The majority of the patriarchal communities (particularly in Africa) tend to extol male virtues while playing down the ability of girls. Besides, girl children and by extension women, face a number of exclusions. Gender identity and its exclusionary potentials for the female are deeply rooted in the fabric of traditional and, sad to say, modern African societies, (Uwakweh, 1998:9). It appears that the said exclusionary potentials are seen as part of the people's culture, so they are taken as the norm and are embedded in all communication instruments, including society's literature, particularly songs and oral narratives. However, accepted as they are, these exclusionary tendencies have far reaching implications, including frustrations which often translate to self defining actions for the girl and later as grown-ups, as observed by Uwakweh (1998). This paper looks at some examples of the oral poetry of the Abakhayo that appear to target the girl child as well as at the responses obtained from face to face interviews with some members of the community, and explores the position of the girl child in the Abakhayo society.

The journey to identity

We want to start tracing the identity of a girl child by considering how the Abakhayo view the girl/female vis-à-vis the male as determined by a juxtaposition of the following poems, selected from many more of the kind but which the limited space of this paper cannot accommodate:

Poem 1

Go slowly/cautiously
Omwana kenda kaala oregumula
Child be cautious lest you trip
Kenda kaala mwana mukhana
Go slowly you are a girl
Kenda kaala oregumula.
Go slowly lest you trip.
Nelikada
She is a reed
Omwana nelikada linafunikha
The child is a fragile reed
Nelikada mwana mukhana
A girl child is a reed
Nelikada linafunikha.
She is a fragile breakable reed.

Poem 2

Samwel Sanya ayala niyemere
Samwel Sanya speaks with authority
Abandu baria
People fear
Musiani wa bakhongo ayala niyemere
Son of the greats speaks with authority
Abandu baria
People fear
Lola Ingwe, lola Isimba niyemere
See the Leopard, see the Lion standing
Abandu baria.
People fear.

It is notable the way the girl in poem 1 is described as fragile and easily breakable, perhaps creating the necessity for her, not just to be cautious about life, but to fear. She should tread slowly and cautiously for fear of tripping, which could be interpreted to mean making the mistakes of life. This is contrasted with the reference to the male, Samwel Sanya in poem 2, as the feared leopard, the feared lion that sends shivers down people's spines whenever he stands up to speak.Indeed it is the metaphor of the fragile, vulnerable woman vis-à-vis that of the man as the indomitable lion that dominates the mind of the growing girl child. Her identity is fraught with images of vulnerability and fear, thus, the attendant need to be protected by the indomitable one. As a reed that easily breaks in the strong winds because of its delicate stem, the girl presumably needs some support for her 'weak' physique and character. Besides, the image of her as a reed sounds quite convenient in view of the fact that society does not allow her to make her own decisions. Like the reed which bends the way the wind blows, society more often than not makes decisions for her, including when and to whom she gets married. As much as the Abakhayo argue that girls these days choose their marriage partners, the pressure on them to get married remains high, as demonstrated in the following poem:

Poem 3

Lanya wekholerere,
LanyaLanya make haste,>
LanyaEwe Lanya wekholerere
Eh, Lanya make haste
Lanya olwo nolukhobo
Lanya this is fore determined
Owomwefwe nokona ano, Lanya
If you delay here my sister, Lanya
Owomwefwe nokona ano
If you delay here my sister
Onalie khunyama embolu.
You will eat stale meat.

Lanya in the above poem is urged to make haste and get married as this is a foregone decision. Perhaps it is a foregone decision because traditionally a girl child belongs to her marital home as we shall see later. Lanya's continued stay in her ancestral home could have dire consequences. She could eat stale meat as suggested in the last line of the poem, and I guess that 'stale meat' here must be something pretty unpleasant. Eating stale meat could perhaps represent being married off to an old man, as is often done to girls who do not get husbands soon enough.The metaphor of fragility and vulnerability is further reinforced by the numerous poems with images of her as a flower: *kano mauwa* (these are flowers); *khuli mauwa* (we are flowers), *Mukhana wefwe neliuwa* (our girl is a flower); and so on. We realize how a flower, though beautiful and treasured, easily wilts and withers in the hot sun. The girl being a flower, seems to suggest immediate need for a 'shade' to protect her from the sun – the man is that shade. Fortunately, her flowery beauty will ensure that she attracts a protector. Away from such stereotypical poems, the girl also hears oral narratives like the popular *Nasio* story in which the ogre takes advantage of the absence of Nasio's brother to eat her. It takes the very brother's heroic act to get her retrieved from the ogre's belly. If only her brother had been around to protect her – the narrative appears to suggest – Nasio would have remained safe. Perpetually exposed to such images, the girl's identity remains incomplete, threatened, or subordinated.

She develops an identity that keeps her appended to a male: brother, father, uncle and even better for the society, a husband, as it is the latter who has to provide her with a permanent abode.

I admit that these references alone cannot of course purport to account for the total identity of the girl child among Abakhayo community. They, however, begin to give a hint on how subordinated and distorted a girl child's identity formation can be. This, on the other hand, could also throw some light on some possible causes of the frustrations alluded to earlier which the girl suffers. It must be frustrating to be in a position where you can't make decisions about your own life.

The promise for belonging

The girl is apparently fully aware that her ancestral place is not her home. This is revealed in the songs that the girl and her colleagues sing on the day of leaving her mother's house for her marital home:

Poem 4

Khuli barende, khuli barende
We are foreigners, we are foreigners
Khuli barende khwechira
Foreigners we now depart
Khuli barende, khuli barende
We are foreigners, we are foreigners
Khuli barende khwechira
Foreigners we now depart
Khulekhere beene esialo
We create room for the land owners
Khuli barende khwechira
Foreigners we now depart
Khulekhere Makokha edala
We allow Makokha to own his home
Khuli barende khwechira.
Foreigners we now depart.

Poem 5

Mubeo ee beene dala
Farewell owners of the homestead
Beene dala mubeo

Owners of the home, farewell
Mubeo ee beene dala.
Farewell owners of the homestead.

Poem 6

Khusebulenge wa beene
We bid farewell
Khusebulenge wa beene
We bid farewell
Abundu ano biri na beene
This place has its owners
Omukeni nomubuyi
A visitor is seasonal
Omukeni nomubuyi
A visitor is seasonal
Omukeni lero luno anauya.

The visitor today will relocate.The three poems: P4, P5 and P6 appear to carry not only the theme of lack of ownership or shareholding, but also surrender. In P4, the girl acknowledges that she is only a foreigner and now the time has come for her to leave her ancestral home for the real owners, particularly for Makokha, her brother. P5 pursues the same theme of leaving space for the real owners of the homestead while P6 emphasizes the fact that the girl was, so to say, only holding a visitor's visa which apparently has expired and she must now relocate.The latter three poems now confirm the identity of the girl child as a temporary member of her father's homestead expressed by the terms 'foreigner' and 'visitor'. For a visitor, terms such as 'depart, farewell, seasonal' and 'relocate' should sound pretty familiar and expected. The terms could be interpreted to carry great significance for the girl who has been socialized to look forward to getting married; first to get a protector and secondly and secondly, to find a permanent home. Presumably, this should be good news for the girl, bearing in mind that every one would be interested in greater sense of belonging, which according to Abakhayo custom the girl's ancestral home cannot provide, but the marital one does – or at least, it is supposed to.

The confirmation that a girl has no place in her father's homestead is found in the community's practice when burying deceased outsiders. If an outsider, that is, a person who is not a member of the family happens to die, his/her remains are buried outside the homestead, preferably in some isolated corner away from the rest of the family. This is how a girl among Abakhayo who fails to get married is buried if she dies while still residing in her father's homestead, implying that she is considered an outsider – an outcast to be precise. Being an outsider, a foreigner, a visitor, and so on, implies that the girl is not only a stranger in her ancestral home, but is also destined to leave when the time comes, since a visitor cannot stay on for ever. This perhaps explains why she is not allocated land or any other property, which as some poems state belong to the owners like Makokha (P4), the girl's brother. The owners in this case are the male members, who our research revealed are called 'abaluyia' – members of the clan, as opposed to 'abakoko' as women are called to mean, outsiders, whose land and property will be found where they permanently belong – the marital home.

'Home at last'

Home at last for the girl journeying to find her identity and belonging sounds quite reassuring. However, her arrival at her 'promised land' and long anticipated home often turns out to be paradoxical. The first signal that the girl could perhaps only be deluding herself about a home in her marital place is read from the interaction between the poem by the girl and her entourage to announce their arrival at the bridegroom's gate and the one that the bridegroom's kin from the other side of the gate respond with. Once at the gate, the girls request to be allowed in, by singing thus:

Poem 7

Munaye ee ee munaye
Riddle eh, eh riddle
Lero njulire
Today I have arrived
Munaye ee ee munaye
Riddle eh, eh riddle
Lero njulire
Today I have arrived
Ekulo ndakonera khumusala
Yesterday I slept perched on a tree
Lero njulire
Today I have arrived
Ekulo ndakonera ewa beene
Where I slept yesterday belongs to its owners
Lero njulire.
Today I have arrived.

On hearing the girls, the bridegroom's kin: aunts, sisters, cousins and others who claim kinship on this side will be heard countering the girls' singing, with the following poem:

Poem 8

Chisike ongore ee!
Locusts of destruction, eh!
Chisike ongore
Locusts of destruction
Chisike ongore chulire
Locusts of destruction have arrived
Chalire ewa Mumia,ee!
They ate at Mumia's, eh!
Chalire ewa Mumia
They ate at Mumia's
Chamalire ewa Mumia, chulire.
They destroyed Mumia's, they have arrived.

The contradictions that arise from the two poems are only too obvious. While the girl sees herself as eventually arriving at her home after what she describes as perching on trees or sleeping in other people's homesteads, her hosts appear to view her as an intruder – a locust of destruction. Evidently, there is neither fair nor homely reception for this girl here. This must be shocking to the girl, who has left her ancestral home with nothing of her own. Indeed with the push by her family to find a husband and the celebration that went with her departure, one would be forgiven to suggest that she was, in fact, being evicted.

The rejection of the girl in her promised land appears sealed with the kind of songs that the bridegroom's kin continues to sing, which include:

Poem 9

Mulekhe seye, ee
Allow me to scorn<
Seye rukhana rufumanga
Scorn the so-called girls of repute
Mulekhe . seye
Allow me to scorn.
Mulekhe nyeke,ee
Allow me to insult
Nyeke rukhana rufumanga
Insult the so-called girls of repute
Mulekhe nyeke.
Allow me to insult.

Poem 10

Omubirangira
The passerby
Lino neliyoni liliburukha
This is a bird that will fly
Mukhasi nomubirangira
A woman is a passerby
Lino neliyoni liliburukha
This is a bird that will fly
Liakwa mungerekha
To land across the river
Lino neliyoni liliburukha
This is a bird that will fly
Liakwa mungerekha
To land across the river
Lino neliyoni liliburukha.
This is a bird that will fly.

Poem 11

Li no nomukeni mubuyi
This is a visitor on the move
Samonyerwa munda<
Who shouldn't be begrudged
Mukhasi nomukeni mubuyi
A woman is a visitor on the move
Samonyerwa munda
Who shouldn't be begrudged

The attack on the girl and her companions in P9 – I guess by the bridegroom's sisters and cousins – scorning her and insulting her, reveals the kind of hostility awaiting her in her promised home. It is also clear from P10 and P11 that even here the girl is seen as an outsider, the same way as she was at her ancestral home. P10 considers her as a passerby, a bird that could fly away any time to land elsewhere, perhaps indicating how much of a temporary member she is considered to be in this home. A bird can hardly be expected to settle in any one spot. Being that temporary in this home – actually a visitor on the move as P11 states – her arrival and stay should not be taken that seriously. There, therefore, will even be no need to allocate her land here. The facts appear to dictate against such a necessity because the girl is seen as everything that discourages any such serious decision: a passerby, a visitor/ guest, and most importantly, an outsider. The 'outsider' metaphor is so much part of the married woman's identity that, in fact, going by the information from our respondents, she is called 'omukwa' (one who fell), perhaps the way rain falls unexpectedly and apparently from nowhere.

Our research also revealed that actually women in the Abakhayo community are not allocated land where they are married. Land can only be owned by a woman's husband or son, which then raises questions about the hopes and promises the girl looked forward to while relocating from her ancestral home – a complete and permanent belonging in her marital home. How will her belonging to her marital place be complete when the situation denies her right to land? How will her belonging be permanent when her new community sees her as a visitor on transit? What then becomes clear is that the girl again misses a definite sense of belonging in her marital home, just as it happened in her ancestral home, where she cannot go back to. And her marital community insists on for ever referring to her by her father's clan or place where she came from – if I may guess – as a way of avoiding to be fully responsible for her. One would again be forgiven to feel that the girl continues to live at her marital place as a kind of squatter, living on land that belongs to the 'owners'.

Citizenship at the national level

Kenya's citizenship policy does not discriminate against women. They get identity cards the same way men do. I suppose that the assumption in awarding this citizenship is that both men and women can enjoy the right to national resources, including land. Indeed Kenya's current constitution stipulates that daughters as much as sons should inherit ancestral land. This provision, however, runs the danger of remaining on pen and paper only while citizenship remains paper citizenship. This hypothesis is informed by the fact that the society's expectations for girl children appear to remain the same: come of age, get married and move out of the father's homestead. Where a girl is going to school, this expectation may be delayed but is expected to come in the long run. Where school is not a factor, this expectation is sooner rather than later.

It is clear from the views I got from the majority of the respondents that the stipulations of the constitution on land inheritance are different from that the one at grassroots level. The reluctance to give girls land appears dressed in cultural, social and economic reasons with some alluding to political and spiritual standpoints. Culturally, some argue, women do not own land – power, privilege, familial lineage and property ownership flow through males and a woman has never been known to own land except when she keeps trusteeship on behalf of her sons in the event of the death of her husband. Socially, a woman leaves her ancestral home and gets married, taking away her whole being. Owning land back at her birth place would only cause divided loyalty, a matter – some argue – that will destabilize marriages, as it gives the woman the options of running back to her inheritance at the slightest excuse.

Arguments against daughters inheriting land get further justification based on what one sees as economic as well as political angles. One of the respondents admitted that he was afraid of being economically overrun by his spouse, who on getting married got the license to till her husband's land, and who, if she got land also from her father, would end up with an economic advantage accruing from this additional property, which – according to what I read in the argument – creates a more economically emancipated woman, who apparently would be difficult to reign in. This fear – as I saw – sounds real as it even touches the very core of the community's politics of control. The men in the community make decisions. The decisions dictate and control what a woman can and cannot do. The mathematics here, however, is that having inherited land at her place of birth – which is outside the jurisdiction of the husband's control – the woman has the sole control over the land, which then makes her a decision maker in her own right. What if she decides to build a house on that land? Wouldn't this affect her loyalty to her marital home and allegiance to her husband?

If the fears and arguments of members of Abakhayo community are not to influence the spirit and fairness of this paper, I would wish to argue – considering the girl's evictee/squatter status – that she is also stateless at national level. So to say, evicted from her ancestral home (consider the push for her to leave and get married), and squatting at her marital home (as she doesn't own land here), the girl remains in a kind of vacuum, which also leaves her empty at national level, even if she is given a national identity card. The national identity card – I wish to argue – only gives her paper citizenship which cannot fulfill full belonging as this is only possible in the presence of the two ingredients of full citizenship: ownership of property and land to live on, both of which the society is hesitant to give to the girl. Indeed, charity begins at home; a landless, stateless individual at the community level does not become a bona fide citizen at national level simply because she has been given paper citizenship, represented by a national identity card.

Conclusion

This paper has discussed the questions of identity and belonging for girl children in patriarchal setups. Studying Abakhayo poems that comment on the girl child to determine how the community views her, the paper has established that the community, whether deliberately or not, seems to train her to look up to the man for support and protection, while looking forward to marriage where she is promised her full sense of belonging, as culturally she has no place in her ancestral home. On getting married, however, the girl faces obstacles in her quest to attain a sense of belonging that she had all along expected to obtain. She finds that just as the case was at her birth place, she cannot get land or be guaranteed a reassuring sense of belonging even at her marital home. She is as much an outsider here as she was at her place of birth – stateless. The paper concludes that the girl's statelessness at the community level renders her stateless at the national level even though she has been issued with a national identity card. Denied ownership of land and other property at the grassroots level even more so, the girl owns nothing at national level, except the national identity card, which, so to say, only grants her mere paper citizenship, therefore, is tantamount to being stateless, anyway.

Works Cited

Alabi, A 'Gender Issues in Zaynab Alkali's Novels', in *Childhood in African Literature.* Ed E Jones, Oxford: James Currey Ltd. 1998.

Kenya Constitution. Nairobi: Government Press, 2010.

Masinjila, M 'Patriarchy', in *Delusions: Essays on Social construction of Gender.* Eds.Kabira, M W; M. Masinjila and W Mbugua. Nairobi: FEMNET, 1994.

Muleka, J, *Images of Women in African Oral Literature.* Deutschland: VDM Verlag Dr Muller. 2009.

Uwakweh, P A, 'Carving a Niche: Visions of Gendered Childhood', in *Childhood in African Literature.* Ed E Jones, Oxford: James Currey Ltd 1998.

Wa Thiong'o, N, 'Literature and Society', in *Teaching of African Literature in Schools.* Eds. E Gachukia and S K Akivaga. Nairobi: KLB. 1978.

12

Some reflections on the endurance of the human spirit in a refugee story

Carey Baraka and Tom Odhiambo

The refugee today

What really happens to a refugee? What does it mean to be suddenly uprooted from one's house, home, village, community or country, and thrown somewhere else unfamiliar? What happens to the human body, mind and spirit when one is forced to leave her family behind, either dead or alive, and have to live in a forest, a camp or new home, with *strangers*? These questions appear mundane. Indeed, unless one has been a refugee, it is probably not worth asking them. But they need to be asked nevertheless. For Kenyans, such questions remain as urgent today as they have been ever since colonialism happened in this country. For when the British appropriated land previously occupied by Africans in the course of setting up a colony here, they created the first group of modern refugees in this country.

Indeed, Kenyans should ask themselves these questions because it continues to host a myriad of refugees. There are thousands of Somalis in Daadab, thousands of South Sudanese in Kakuma, where are to be found Ethiopians, Eritreans, Congolese, Ugandans etc. Then there are the 'refugees' who no longer can be called so because they have *become* Kenyans after years of integrating. And just as a question to ponder, why are we sending back to Somalia people who, for all intents and purpose, are Kenyans? What would it cost us materially, socially, culturally or politically to naturalize the refugees in the camps as Kenyans?

Maybe these are idle questions considering that we have the refugees we would rather not *see*, *hear* about or *feel* for: our own internally displaced persons. These are the human beings with whom we share humanity, nationality, culture, politics, religion; people with whom we belong together but whom we have converted into a mere phrase, the IDPs and normalized as a statistic. And this is the main problem with being a refugee. These days refugees seem not to find the *refuge* that they sought in the first place when they run away from home. They are simply a number that can be represented graphically, wracked by hunger, disease and insecurity. Yet, they survive.

That is why we should be asking: how do refugees live their tragic lives. What kind of relationship is forged between the refugee and his/her host community? What circumstances, in the host community make it possible for the refugee to survive, for one more day? Is it just the kindness of his/her hosts? Or is it something in the person of the refugee, the *human spirit*, which he shares with those among whom he lives that enables sustenance of life? Could this human endurance be something to be *shared*, between the refugee and his/her new community, and therefore enable a better understanding of the world; and possibly offer opportunity for a more *humane* world?

The story of Habineza and Vestine, two refugees from Rwanda, and their children, as told in the novel *The Ghosts of 1894* by Oduor Jagero, can point us to ways of seeing the refugee's situation. This is a story of pain, suffering but also endurance. It is a story of previously 'peaceful' lives jolted by the Rwandan crisis of 1994, life in the mayhem of those 100 or so murderous days; a refuge in Kenya and subsequent displacement by Kenya's own political and refugee crisis of 2007/2008.

This is what happens in *The Ghosts of 1894*. Habineza is born a Tutsi, although his paternal grandmother was Hutu. But when growing up, there were really no Hutu or Tutsi. There were just Banyarwanda. Remembering his life, he narrates,

> When I was born my father gave me the name Habineza. Habineza was his grandfather, an honorable Tutsi man who kept large herds of cattle and beat the odds as one of the few Tutsis who farmed. Once when the village was in hunger he gave half of his produce to the village. Everyone sang his name. He married a Hutu. It would be a big deal when I was born. But back then itwas not. We were Banyarwanda. We traded milk and meat for farm produce. If we were attacked, we defended as Banyarwanda. We died as Banyarwanda and we were buried as Banyarwanda (102).

But it is not long before Habineza and his parents are forced to migrate to Uganda when their Hutu neighbours turn against them. He grows up there but eventually the family returns to settle in Kigali only for the crisis of 1994 to force him out of Kigali and Rwanda before he *returns* in 2008. The one enduring question to ask is: Is Habineza and his kind fated to this cycle of violence and displacement? And if this unending drama of violence, death and dislocation is a permanent feature of his life, how has he endured it and what lessons can we learn from this story? It seems that Habineza's survival is built on three elements, among others. These are: an undying sense of belonging; a spirit of friendship; and a capacity for solidarity.

On belonging

Habineza seems to have a strong sense of attachment to Rwanda, his family and his community. The brief story of his birth, cited above, suggests that this is a man who acknowledges his mixed heritage. Although 'official' identification makes him a Tutsi, he knows that he has Hutu blood coursing through him. This makes him a Munyarwanda. His people are Banyarwanda, those who belong to Rwanda. He is aware that his physique does not determine who he is and how he relates to others in his country. It is the *being* together with fellow Banyarwanda, speaking the *same* language, *Kinyarwanda,* that makes him one with the others in the community.

This natural attribute of humanity, this ability to speak with others, to share experiences of life and world views, is what makes people belong to places and with other people. This is why in the heat of the violence in Kigali, a captain in the United Nations Mission in Rwanda (UNAMIR) tells the leader of a killer gang at a road blockade, "Surely there must be a better way to do that?" The leader replied, "Show me another way." The Captain's answers, "Dialogue sir. Dialogue makes the difference!" But the man is obstinate and insists, "There is the language of the UN, soldier, and there is the human language. Barbaric and stupid though it is, the human language accomplishes miracles."

Indeed, to speak of belonging is the foremost function of human language. A child cries when born to declare its presence and claim its place in the world. So do human beings declare shared humanity when they introduce themselves or greet others. We alienate, we declare as non- belonging or un-belonging when we emphasize the difference between us rather than celebrate the shared humanity. Indeed it is this shared humanity that Habineza's story highlights most to us when he says this after his family's arrival in Uganda, "The people on the other side looked at us with curiosity: who were we? Where had we come from and what were we running away from? I think *they somehow realized that we were just like them.* We ate the same cassava and yams and squatted in the bush just like they did. So they empathized with us" [our italics]. It is the knowledge of the possibility for empathy even in foreign lands that makes life manageable for Habineza. And this has always been the refugees sense of belonging; belonging to one's natal place but also belonging to the bigger world out there.

On friendship

As Habineza tells us above, that he thought the people among whom his family had decided to settle 'somehow realized that we were just like them', he makes a profound statement about the source of friendship. If being a refugee is due to violence and forced dislocation, then it is just as well due to loss of the possibilities for friendship. To seek refuge in a strange land, among people one does not know or had known about but had never interacted or lived with, and in new climes is to at the same time test the possibilities for friendship.

But what does friendship mean and how do people become friends? What do we mean when we say so and so is my friend? All human societies have the idea and practice of friendship. But as Daniel Schwartz reminds us:

> In the Aristotelian tradition, fellow soldiers, fellow travellers, and fellow citizens are friends, as are those who interact with a view to utility and those whose bond is founded on erotic love. Indeed, it would seem that almost anyone who is not an enemy, and is in some way engaged in a more or less stable and mutually beneficial relationship, is a friend. In contrast, the modern concept seems to apply to a smaller number of people. We tend to call friends those persons (usually not relatives) with whom we have a substantial degree of closeness and intimacy. Persons situated in more distant circles of interaction are regarded as friends only by stretching the reach of the term. (2007: 2)

It is the friendship of the people of Uganda that sustains Habineza – and thousands of fellow Rwandese – when they are forced to migrate there. But of most significance is that Habineza says that when he married his wife – Rosy, who is killed in the early days of the genocide – he gained a sense of direction in his life. In other words, the friendship with his wife gave him purpose and direction.

Again, it is his friendship with Vestine, a fellow victim of the genocide, which sustains him throughout the period of the violence. They invest trust in each other and forge a common bond. Vestine becomes the friend that his wife was before, and indeed becomes his wife later in life after they had resettled in Kenya.

Ghosts of 1894 offers several instances when friendship provides succour for those in hardship. Habineza survives the tragedy of his life because of several friends: Vestine, an American journalist; Sandra; Maina and Korir in Eldoret, Kenya; etc. His living child, Akamanzi, and Vestine's daughter, Juliet, also partly survive the genocide through their friendship with a gorilla that they name 'Buddy', and their time together with an American couple, Lee and Petra. The ties of friendship guarantee companionship, sharing and a sense of sanity and life.

On solidarity

It is friendship that provides the ground on which solidarity is built. Solidarity is about obligation to other human beings. It is about extending a helping hand, sharing in the troubles as well as joys of others but most important in acknowledging our being part of a larger group. Group solidarity is about the degree of shared responsibility when one belongs. *Undugu,* a term that our politicians love, is not just about fraternity, it is about accepting that even those we do not share immediate blood kinship with, we share *some* togetherness with them. Solidarity enables us to see beyond our immediate and private needs, and instead see these needs as shared in one way or another.

But solidarity can sometimes be discovered to be set on weak grounds when tested by forces of alienation, violence and destruction like genocide. In the context of the story of *Ghosts of 1894,* the solidarity in Habineza's village is destroyed when the imagined differences between the members of the community is privileged over what is common to all. Being Hutu or Tutsi suddenly separates one individual from the other. The consequence is erasure of trust, togetherness and belonging. Friends become enemies; relatives become strangers to each other; and the community can no longer speak, act or share as one. In such a world, the group can no longer pursue similar goals. Suspicion, fear and distrust reign and become the catalyst for violence.

Consequently a child, a woman, a man or a group can no longer be the same thing. As Habineza cries, although in this context questioning his faith in God, "I'm confused. I once believed, because there was a reason to believe. There was peace; there was friendship … brotherhood. Humans were humans. Men were men and women were women. Children were children" (40). Because the shared belongingness is ruptured, children become killers of their parents and friends, women turn into murderers of their spouses and children and men simply burn down the country.

It is therefore imperative that when we talk about identity, nationalism, belonging etc, that we remember how unstable these ideas are. As ideas, it is probable to talk about them with certainty, even finality. But as lived experiences, to paraphrase Oduor Jagero, these are like ghosts, often capable of unravelling without forewarning. Refugees are proof of the weakness of these categories. To be a refugee is to negotiate belonging, homeliness, nationality, personhood or your humanity every day. For those who are not refugees, probably the task is to creatively but also proactively work at how to make it possible for all humanity to not only think of belonging but actually *belong* securely.

References

Jagero, Oduor. 2016. *The Ghosts of 1894.* Nairobi: KoaMedia.
Schwartz, Daniel. 2007. *Aquinas on Friendship.* Oxford: Oxford University Press.

13.

Journey out of the state of statelessness: Kenya's unfinished business

Wandia Njoya

I was initially meant to submit an article about references to Rwanda, and specifically the genocide against the Tutsi in 1994, in Kenyan discussions about ethnicity and identity.

However, when I got to the *Samosa* festival colloquium jointly organized by *Awaaz Magazine* and the Department of Literature of the University of Nairobi, I found a conversation different from the one that I had anticipated. A few days later, when I tried to complete the article I originally had in mind, I lost a friend who was an integral part of my conversation about identity in the Kenyan landscape. I had no choice but to change my manuscript.

This paper is a tribute to my friend Adam Hussein Adam, a man who lived as a victim of the Kenyan state's use of ethnicity to ostracize large segments of the population from fully participating as citizens in national life. I tell more than just a story about two friends; I also talk about a struggle to mainstream discussions of the political dimensions of ethnicity in Kenyan intellectual discourse. Since before independence, culture has maintained a strong grip on continental African discussions of identity, even when, I argue, attention to the political dimensions is more urgent. What is interesting, though, is that this tension between the political and cultural considerations of identity emerged in discussions of identity Frantz Fanon, a black man from Martinique, and the African intellectuals who attended the Second Congress of Black Writers and Artists in Rome in 1959. Fanon recorded his thoughts on the subject in his last publication *The Wretched of the Earth*. Interestingly enough, the same difference in perspective emerged in this last forum of the 2016 edition of the SAMOSA festival.

Reconnection

In his welcome address to participants of the forum, Zahid Rajan, one of the founders of the SAMOSA Festival, said that the forum was a culmination of conversations going on in Eastleigh, a community that has repeatedly suffered state and criminal violence, which is, in turn, institutionally reinforced by denial of ID cards to people largely of Somali origin. Denial of ID cards means systematic disenfranchisement, because without the card, one cannot get a SIM card, cannot transact on mobile money platforms such as MPESA or open a bank account, or get admission into tertiary educational institutions. In such an environment, discussion of voters' cards appears almost as frivolous as the politicians who obsess about it.

Prof. Yash Pal Ghai, the keynote speaker, stirred our thinking about citizenship by telling us how the constitution was meant to entrench a Kenyan identity that embraced the history and humanity of the different peoples who have settled in this territory over the last two centuries. He was followed by Aleya Kassam, a wonderful writer whose passion and soul are so infused in her writing, that she is a delight to listen to.

As all these people spoke, I shared snippets of the conversations on Twitter and Facebook. Within minutes, notifications on Facebook started pouring in. My friend Adam Hussein was posting comments on my updates. In the conversation that followed, I eventually said: 'I see I've touched a topic close to your heart. We need to reconnect.' And he replied, 'We must connect! I participated in the SAMOSA Festival in Eastleigh. One thing emerged – people are tired of looking for documents that are not being issued. They are arrested and harassed with or without documents.'

The connection Adam and I were talking about was a long standing promise that we would continue our conversations about marginalization. The plan began when Adam and I met in 2012 at a seminar I offered on African political thought, which I opened to the public. The purpose of the class was to provide tools, in addition to ethnicity, that can be used to discuss politics. It was during our discussions that Adam shared his story of how difficult it was to integrate in Kenyan society, because he could not get official government documents, for the simple reason that he was Nubian. Later that year, I invited Adam to speak to my students about the structure of marginalization (Njoya, 2012). Since then, Adam and I had talked about organizing a lengthier program with the goal of mainstreaming such conversations in academia. But the reconnection with Adam was never to be. Just a week after the SAMOSA Festival colloquium, Adam passed away. He suffered a heart attack, and by the time he arrived at the hospital, it was too late. He left behind unfinished business.

Ethnicity as both political and cultural

My conversations with Adam about marginalization are pertinent because of the way the discussions at the University of Nairobi forum progressed. Towards the end of the day, we seemed to be stagnating in a cliché conversation about culture and identity. That cliché basically goes like this: we should be proud of our specific ethnic groups, so that we all have something to share at the table of diversity that is Kenya. Towards the end of the forum, I voiced my frustration with this repeat conversation, asking: must identity only be ethnic? The human being has a multifaceted identity. We're ethnic, professional, geographical, family, citizen, ad infinitum. Why don't we talk about our other identities, I asked?

And then came the response that simply reinforced the suffocating nature of the diversity talk. One response, in particular, came in the form of testing my authority to speak, through naming areas and asking if I'd been there. I'd been to some, but not others. Then I was told: people from regions outside Nairobi identify themselves as ethnic groups. It is mainly people from Nairobi who do not want to be identified with a particular ethnic group.

I erupted because I understood where that conversation was headed, which was to the argument that I am a spoiled, rootless Nairobi brat, too colonized to know my roots. I had listened so many times before to the ethnic-diversity question to know that when anyone questions it, the response is to imply that the question comes from colonial alienation from the speaker's African roots.

So in reply, I asked: what is the point of us celebrating our weddings, initiation ceremonies, songs and proverbs, if we can't get IDs, title deeds and other official documents? I drew the example from my experience of working in Kwale, where the local community is so disenfranchised that the area has become the home of the Mombasa Republican Council (MRC). Besides, Prof Ghai had told us earlier in the day that as he wrote the initial draft of the new constitution, one of the queries he got from his legal colleagues was why the constitution gave very elaborate details on who is a Kenyan citizen, and on the right of every citizen to a 'Kenyan passport and any document of registration or identification issued by the state to citizens.' His reply was that he had to be that elaborate, because identity is such a hot button issue in Kenya.

Later that evening, I vented my frustration with the diversity conversation by posting this on Facebook:

> Now, this sentimentalism of saying we are proud of our ethnic groups, ati so we're embracing diversity, just doesn't work for me. Don't tell me you're proud of your ethnicity if you tell people you want to be president of Kenya, and everyone gives you that 'are you stupid' smile, because of your ethnicity. Or if you can't get an ID or passport because some ignorant civil servant tells you that your great great grandparent was not born in Kenya, as if Kenya existed then. Or if you're a squatter on your ancestral land and can't get a title deed. The issue isn't whether we're proud

of our ethnicities, which I'm sure many of us are. The issue is why the Republic of Kenya isn't proud enough of it to honour your constitutional right to identity and other official documents, and proud enough to enable you to live in dignity in any corner of this Kenya.

Making the above distinction between ethnicity as politics and ethnicity as culture is very difficult in Kenyan conversations; any time one wants to talk about how the instruments of the state have created economic disparities along ethnic lines, the standard reply is that we should be proud of our diversity of cultures. Therein lies the incoherence of identity questions in Kenyan public discourse: we respond to political problems with cultural solutions. And we repeat it year after year after year, in the hope that if we can shout loud enough 'tunajivuniakuwawakenya,' sing some of our folk songs, praise #TeamKenya and promote tourism, the incoherence will go away. But it does not.

I was not surprised when one comment on that post on diversity suggested that the problem is not hate but corruption in the civil service. I replied that such responses mean little to people like my friend Adam and his family who cannot get ID cards. In reply, the commentator asked, 'What do you suggest?' Adam then replied: 'While all Kenyans have rights, the right of other Kenyans requires a guarantee from those who enjoy theirs. In this case, those who can't get ID cards need those who have IDs to stand up for them.' Adam's response, I said, was the real diversity. It was real because it comes from a political and social consciousness, not from simply comparing and contrasting how different ethnic groups speak, dance, eat and marry.

This was not the first time I was trying – albeit unsuccessfully – to make that distinction. In the African political thought class in which Adam participated, I tried to differentiate ethnicity as politics from ethnicity as culture, and I did so by leading a discussion about Frantz Fanon's similar frustrations. Writing his last book, *The Wretched of the Earth,* as he battled leukemia, Fanon could see that African nationalists would make a grave mistake if they confused the politics of race with the culture of different ethnicities. In his chapter on 'The trials and tribulations of national consciousness,' he strongly cautioned African nationalists against adopting the colonial cultural framework of dishing out power and resources based on skin color and cultural identity, all under the banner of 'Africanization,' instead of adopting a national identity bases on social and political consciousness. He argued that the temptation to focus on culture, rather than consciousness, would make African leaders simply replace white skins in government with black ones. That simplistic reasoning would, in turn, trickle down to the masses, who would perpetuate the same bigotry through ethnicity. He illustrated his argument as follows:

In the Ivory Coast, outright race riots were directed against the Dahomeans and Upper Voltans [present day Beninois and Burkinabes] who controlled much of the business sector and were the target of hostile demonstrations by the Ivorians following independence. We have switched from nationalism, to ultranationalism, chauvinism and racism. There is a general call for these foreigners to leave, their shops are burned, their market booths torn down and some are lynched; consequently, the Ivorian government orders them to leave, thereby satisfying the demand of the nationals. In Senegal, it was the anti-Sudanese [Malian] demonstrations... (103-104).

This ethnic scramble for the colonial loot left behind at independence replicated itself across Africa. The major problem, Fanon said, was that African leaders were not rooted in 'a genuine endeavor at nationalization' and they instead settled for the mere 'transfer of power previously held by the foreigners, [and] the masses make the very same demand at their own level' (104). Once this situation is entrenched, the difference between nationalist chauvinism and tribalism is 'but one small step' (105).The African countries would rapidly slide into tribalism because African leaders had failed to enlighten 'the people as a whole' or 'put the people first,' which, in turn, was due to the national bourgeoisie's 'petty-mindedness' and lack of ideological clarity (106). Fanon was essentially saying that national identity could not be constructed on pre-colonial identities and skin color; it had to be ideologically and politically constructed. That is not to say that an ethnic group is pre-colonial; it is to say, that the ethnic group should not be defined by its precolonial terms. That means that in the Kenyan nation, people like the Nubian, the Indian and the Makonde, must not be defined by Sudan, India and Mozambique where they came from two hundred years ago. Their histories of arrival in Kenya, their contributions to the nation, some of which we can anecdotally cite as Kibra, as masala and chapatti as Kenyans' staple diets, and as carving skills which were later adopted by the Kamba craftsmen and are now an integral part of our craft exports and the tourist experience, must be counted as what makes these groups Kenyan. And when one thinks of it, the same principle also applies to other Kenyan 'mainstream' tribes who are often faulted as being visitors when they settle in areas where they did not originally live three centuries ago.

Fanon calls this process a deliberate construction of a national identity through 'a social and political consciousness' (142). This consciousness is, in turn, built through what Fanon calls 'the minds and muscles of the men and women' (143), which is created through education, work, knowledge of the struggles of other oppressed peoples worldwide, and a national conversation on 'not only an economic program but also a policy on the distribution of wealth and social relations.' He adds that in all these efforts, the bottom line is our human identity, and concludes: 'If nationalism is not explained, enriched and deepened, if it does not very quickly turn into a social and political consciousness, into humanism, then it leads to a dead end' (144).

To a large extent, Yash Pal Ghai (2016) does the same thing as Fanon by distancing identity from pre-colonial boundaries. While Fanon does so in an economic and political framework, Ghai does it in a legal one. As he drafted the new constitution, Prof Ghai envisioned it as constructing a new Kenyan identity, which in the context of Kenya's ethnically polarized landscape, is quite a radical idea. As he explains, the constitution broadens the idea of Kenyan identity by expanding diversity to religion and culture, and defining us by our common aspirations and our essential values of 'human rights, equality, freedom, democracy, social justice and the rule of law.' In other words, we may ethnically be the same people as some centuries ago, but we can politically, socially, legally and economically redefine our identities and our relationships across cultures and regions.

By contrast, the conversation which I found frustrating confined identity to culture and traditions. Ghai noted it too, but in contrast to my impatience, he patiently distinguished the peculiarity as follows: 'A major difference between the scholarly and the lawyers' approaches that struck me was that the scholar studies identity as it defines a community or group, while a lawyer's major interest is often the shaping of identity—of the nation and the people.'

Mainstreaming conversations on statelessness

What fascinated me about Adam Hussein was that he was probably the first Kenyan whom I heard making that distinction between political and cultural ethnicity. Adam understood that certain ethnic groups were marginalized, and not by their culture, or by prejudice alone. His experience as a fourth-generation Kenyan of Nubian heritage made it clear to him that the discrimination against Nubians was entrenched by the state. As he says in several interviews and essays, he lost the opportunity to play in the Kenya rugby team, and lost opportunities for work, because the Kenyan state does not recognize Nubians as a Kenyan ethnic group. He was able to get his ID card only by virtue of having studied at the elite national Kabarak High School, but his siblings would wait for between eleven and sixteen years for their ID cards (Adam, 2010). Nevertheless, it took Adam 10 years to finally get employed, because prospective employers asked him for a pile of documents that other 'mainstream' ethnic groups are not asked for (McKenzie, 2011).

I treasured Adam's friendship. Adam consoled me that I was not crazy to think about ethnicity the way I did, and that I was not simply a colonized Nairobi brat. Every time we bumped into each other, we talked at length about the need for Kenyans to understand that some of our people have genuine complaints about ethnic discrimination, and that that was not an accusation against favoured ethnic groups but against the state. So at the end of 2012, I invited Adam to talk about marginalization to our university community. At the time, I had dreams that Kenyans could be taught to think politically and socially, and having a talk by Adam would be a start.

But it wasn't that easy.

When I was pinning the posters around, some of the faculty responded with a skeptical question about why anyone on earth would call themselves marginalized, and even whether marginalization actually exists in Kenya. My response was, well, come listen to Adam and find out for yourself. But when the day came, we were an audience of about five. I was embarrassed, but Adam told me not to worry; five was good enough.

And when it became clear why, I was blown away.

Adam truly believed in Kenya and believed that Kenyans from 'mainstream' tribes would do the right thing. He felt that if he could tell one more Kenyan to care about the marginalized, he had made a difference. He was not bitter, despite all that he had been through. He was hopeful. He told us that the majority can guarantee the rights of minorities, since the majority has the clout and presence which minorities don't have. 'If the majority does not desire justice,' he said, 'the minority will suffer.' But even if he appealed to the conscience of the majority, he nevertheless warned that the majority's silence would force the minority to take up arms (Njoya, 2012). As it so happened, around that time, Kenya was reeling from shock following the death of forty-two police officers sent to quell inter-ethnic violence in Baragoi in Samburu, with one newspaper calling the region the 'Wild North' (Gisesa and Letiwa, 2012). After Adam had shared his story, the students present expressed surprise at how little they knew about the plight of minorities, and how the media grossly misrepresented northern Kenya.

But Adam did not mock their ignorance. Instead, he challenged them to consider writing more accurate stories about the region.

After that day in November 2012, it was clear to us that there was need to mainstream the conversations about marginalization. We kept promising each other that we'd organize a whole day event when students would be exposed to the politics, culture and economy of the marginalized areas. The following year, I asked Adam if he was interested in us doing a panel together on ethnicity and marginalization at the International Interdisciplinary Conference at the Catholic University of East Africa. He enthusiastically took up the challenge, sending me his abstracts and allowing me to edit and show him the process of submission. Our presentations in June 2013 went really well.

But that was the last major thing we did together. I was swept away by my administrative duties, and Adam enrolled as a PhD student in Clinical Psychology at Daystar University. Our being in the same institution didn't give us the time to finally accomplish our dream – we just bumped into each other, said quick hellos and went on to other things. We did not talk much again until that Facebook chat on the SAMOSA Festival Forum.

Unfinished business

When Njonjo Mue, a mutual friend to Adam and I, called me one morning a week later and gave me the news, I was devastated. I told my husband about the loss of this great friend of mine, and then posted a tribute on Facebook where I talked about how I was amazed by Adam's genuineness and faith in Kenya, a Kenya that had let him down. I apologized so profusely that we never got the time to organize the meetings we had talked about for three years. As the comments trickled in, the common thread in the posts and comments was about Adam's openness and genuineness, and the fact that he had left behind work that we had not yet completed. Njonjo remembered our African political thought class and wrote, 'You were so authentic in everything you did.' In her comment on my post, my friend Michelle said that she was, in fact, supposed to meet Adam the day before he died: 'We were to meet yesterday with Adam; he postponed the meeting, told me he was unwell and resting. I'm sad and shocked to hear this news. He is a magnificent soul.' Another friend, Stephen, said in a different post: 'So sad you had to leave before we actualized our discussion at Capital Centre.' In my opinion, some of the most memorable words came from Judy Kimamo. In reply to my post, she wrote: 'I also have a bunch of unfinished business with him. I too, am sorry I got too busy. But this morning I felt his presence and yet again I failed to call or message him ... now this. We will pursue what he proposed as the journey out of this state of statelessness.' On her wall, she said, 'It's very hard to believe this; we had many plans together. You gave me courage, through words and thought to face life every day, no matter the challenge.'

It is evident that Adam brought together a diverse group of people through his openness, his generosity, and the welcome he extended to everyone to participate in 'the journey out of this state of statelessness.' In this way, he modeled the Kenya he and many of us want to see, a Kenya where identity is constructed politically, economically, legally, socially, culturally and ideologically, not just on outdated colonial boundaries. But Adam did not live to see his dream come true.

May Adam rest in peace. The best tribute that we Kenyan intellectuals, especially in literature studies, can give Adam and many Kenyans like him, is to speak for those whose voice is taken from them, the way Adam believed that we could. Unlike the suggestion at the colloquium, I do not believe that Nairobians wondering why every identity discussion must revolve around ethnicity is the real bourgeois conversation; rather, it is to be found with academics confining ethnicity to culture and ignoring the millions of Kenyans, the Makonde, Nubians, Asians and Somalis whose ethnicity is used by the state to exclude them from full Kenyan citizenship. I believe that academics should use their intellectual tools to complete the unfinished business of reconstructing a new Kenya, the Kenya which my friend Adam, the SAMOSA Festival, and so many other Kenyans, aspire for.

Works cited

Adam, Hussein Adam. Tragedies of the Stateless.Open Society Foundations, 20

Sept. 2010, https://www.opensocietyfoundations.org/voices/tragedies-stateless. Accessed 10 Aug. 2016 Fanon, Frantz. The Wretched of the Earth.Trans. Richard Philcox. New York: Grove, 2004.

Ghai, Yash Pal. 'The Law Aims to Give Every Kenyan Sense of Belonging.' The Star, 30 June 2016, http://www.the-star.co.ke/news/2016/07/30/the-law-aims-to-give-every-kenyan-sense-of-belonging_c1394037?page=0%2C0. Accessed 10 Aug. 2016.

Gisesa, Nyambega and Paul Letiwa. 'Kenya's Wild North.' Daily Nation, 19 Nov. 2012, http://www. nation.co.ke/Features/DN2/Kenyas-Wild-North/-/957860/1623312/-/m0g14c/-/index. html. Accessed 10 Aug. 2016.

McKenzie, David. 'Kenya's Nubians: Outsiders in Their Own Country.' CNN, 4 May 2011, http:// edition.cnn.com/2011/WORLD/africa/05/04/kenya.nubian.discrimination/. Accessed 10 Aug. 2016.

Njoya, Wandia. 'Every Kenyan Should Fight Marginalization.' 14 Nov. 2012, https:// sites.google.com/a/daystar.ac.ke/department-of-language-and-performing-arts/what-we-do/everykenyanshouldfightmarginalisation. Accessed 10 Aug. 2016.

14

Exile and identity: Representations of trauma in Warsan Shire's refugee poems: Souvenir and Home

Lynda A Ouma

Introduction

The theme of exile and search for identity has engaged the imagination of writers in recent times from personal experience or implicitly. While some are forced to leave home due to unavoidable circumstances such as war or fear of persecution, others move out of choice in search of greener pastures. Refugee writing from Africa addresses the disillusionment with life in the host countries and of late, focus has been on the dissatisfaction with the way refugees and asylum seekers are treated the world over. According to Edward Said in his essay *Reflections on Exile* (2012), 'Exile is strangely compelling to think about but terrible to experience'. He adds that

> It is the unhealable rift forced between a human being and a native place, between the self and its true home: its essential sadness can never be surmounted. And while it is true that literature and history contain heroic, romantic, glorious, even triumphant episodes in an exile's life, these are no more than efforts meant to overcome the crippling sorrow of estrangement. The achievements of exile are permanently undermined by the loss of something left behind forever. (137).

The anxiety and loss described by Said above is reminiscent in the poetry of Warsan Shire, who in an interview with the *Guardian* stated that she wrote the poem *Conversations About Home, (at the Deportation Centre),* to highlight the experiences of those who have gone through the grief and trauma of fleeing their homeland.

Refugee choices

Shire's poetry explores the unimaginable choices that refugees must make as they look for safer spaces and highlights the struggles that result with these choices. Her poetry allows readers to experience and empathise with the trauma manifested through anxiety, pain and loss of identity that come with displacement. Herein we see the important role that literature plays in creatively illuminating the struggles of the vulnerable in society and reordering the facts of life making them clearer.

Eastern Africa and especially the Horn of Africa are both a source and home of the world's largest population of refugees and internally displaced people. Kenya has the unenviable distinction of hosting the world's biggest refugee camp, Daadab, in the North-Eastern part of the country. As of May 2016, the Kenyan government announced that plans were underway to close the camp by November 2016, a decision that could displace more than 500,000 persons who know no other home. This refugee scenario calls for an examination of how literature highlights the plight of refugees in an effort to seek solutions and highlight the critical role art plays in dealing with difficult circumstances. This paper examines *Souvenir* and *Conversations About Home (At the Deportation Centre)*, poems by Warsan Shire from the collection *Our Men Do Not Belong to Us* (2014), to highlight the plight of refugees.

The theoretical perspective

I engage the formalist theoretical perspective in examining the poems to bring out their aesthetic function. This theory is concerned with the formal elements of a text and would have a reader understand and value a work for its own inherent worth, not for its service to metaliterary matters. The importance of yielding meaning from a work is further emphasized by Chinua Achebe in his essay, *The truth of fiction*, in which he contrasts beneficent fiction with malignant fiction. He designates the former as a literary function due to its imaginative nature that enables the writer to go beyond time and place and suggest a kind of humanism thereby giving us the moral ideal. By its nature literature transcends a way of life of a people and presents us with something better and moral. Formalist theoretical perspective thus respects the autonomy of literature.

I also endeavour to highlight the sociological impact of literature in the society. To this end I am concerned with the problems that affect refugees which are, but not limited to, loss of identity, loneliness, longing for and search for home, dehumanization and the trauma that results from surviving civil unrest.

Memory, Trauma and Identity

Harrowing events such as genocide, war, terrorism, civil and ethnic strife often generate serious and often catastrophic challenges to communal self-understandings, the 'memory' of such 'traumas' play a significant and sometimes elemental role in shaping subsequent political perceptions, affiliations and action. That is according to Duncan Bell in the introductory comments to the book *Memory, Trauma and World Politics* (2006:5). One can thus see a connection between memory, trauma and identity of an individual. In moments of crisis Bell further states that 'we tend to look back into the past with intensity to draw on and reshape our memories in an effort to defend challenged identities and shore up a sense of self and community' (6).

The human body is focused on as the site where representations of identity are inscribed. Bell explores the tensions between the refugees' lived bodily experiences and the meanings inscribed to it. The author articulates this through a vivid description of an obsolete passport being destroyed at an airport; the use of extended metaphor here suggests the internalising of the process of identity crisis. In stanza one, she says, 'I tore up and ate my own passport in an airport hotel. I'm bloated with language I can't afford to forget' (24). The next stanza continues, 'They ask me how did you get here? Can't they see it on my body? The Libyan desert red with immigrant bodies, the Gulf of Aden bloated, the city of Rome with no jacket'(25). Here the body complete with scars of the journey becomes the immigrants canvas which carries the answers to the riddle of identity and also provides the history and justification for the struggle. Refugees fleeing into Kenya from the Horn of Africa have a similar story to tell, they may not cross oceans but the situation they encounter at border points presents a loss of identity as they adopt refugee status in order to secure a chance at getting asylum. The connection between memory and identity is further highlighted in the opening lines of *Souvenir* where the poet speaks of the act of bringing the war with you and it being in your blood as if it were part of your DNA; 'you brought the war with you unknowingly, perhaps on your skin, in hurried suitcases, in photographs, plumes of it in your hair, under your nails, maybe it was in your blood' (22). Embodiment here is thus used as a strategy to highlight the disruption of normal social life.

The feelings of loneliness, longing for home are brought out in the opening stanza of the poem *Home*, an abridged version of the poem *Conversations About Home (At the Deportation Centre)*, with the hauntingly powerful lines 'no one leaves home unless home is the mouth of a shark'. This paints a picture of an unwelcoming environment which they must flee from. This thought of mass flight is developed throughout the poem where the poet speaks of the whole city running for the border. The persona explores conditions under which one would leave home in the fourth stanza, *'no one would leave home unless home chased you, fire under feet, hot blood in your belly'*. This idiomatic expression extends the idea of flight, with the choice of words aptly conveying the pain and discomfort experienced when one leaves home, a place familiar to them for an unknown destination and its uncertainties. This longing and desire for home coupled with a sense of loss is repeated in the tenth and final stanzas of the poem *Home*. Refugees live in a state of limbo, they no longer have a home to go back to and their new home after sometime proves unwelcoming. Life in the camps is not ideal nor is it easy but they do not have the luxury of going back home because they have no home to go to, country is ravaged by war, home is the barrel of a gun. They are faced with the sad reality of having left behind loved ones who they will probably not see again.

This unhomely world depicted in the poem *Home* is the reality of refugees which media organisations have captured time and again. The Integrated Regional Information Networks (IRIN) News in 2011 documented the experience of Moulid Iftin Hujale who has lived in Dadaab refugee camp since he was ten years old. In an article written for IRIN News website he says;

> I am embarrassed when I'm forced to introduce myself as "a Somali refugee living in Kenya". I am no longer in Somalia and yet I am not a Kenyan citizen; so where do I belong? Am I going to be a refugee for ever? I feel I am lost in between. (irinnews.org).

A feeling of imprisonment compounds this sense of statelessness. The eighth stanza lines 6 to 10 of *Home* advances the thought that the refugee is welcome in the host country but with limited freedom.

> lose your name, lose your family, make a refugee camp a home for a year or two or ten, stripped and searched, find prison everywhere and if you survive and you are greeted on the other side with go home blacks.

The free verse here points to the angst experienced by refugees residing in camps. Moulid Iftin Hujale mentioned earlier continues to say in his interview with IRIN News that, 'One of the biggest challenges the youth face in the camp is the restriction of movement. I hate looking for a travel document just to go outside the camp. The encampment policy has crippled our potential. I feel I am in prison' (irinnews.org).

Further challenges experienced by refugees include dehumanization and the psychological trauma of dealing with memories of war. Many children lose their innocence as they are recruited to join the warring armies. The third stanza lines two to five of *Home* raises alarm over this rising phenomenon;
the boy you went to school with
who kissed you dizzy behind
the old tin factory is
*holding a gun bigger than his body*The poet engages our human senses in articulating the psychological trauma of escaping war. This serves to situate the reader in the experiences of the refugee subject as they flee their homeland. In

Souvenir we observe that the war and memories of it are ever present for the refugee. The images and memories of the devastating effects follow the refugee in their new home and are presented as being a part of their life which they cannot shake off. Stanza three lines seven to twelve:

> the war lies between you and your partner in the bed stands behind you at the bathroom sink even the dentist jumped back from the wormhole of your mouth. You suspect it was probably the war he saw, so much blood (22).

From the third stanza we see that images of war are persistent in the mind of the refugee. The fourth stanza continues this idea by saying:

> You know peace like someone who has survived a long war, take it one day at a time because everything has the scent of a possible war; you know how easily a war can start one moment quiet, next blood.

From the above it is evident that the refugee's state of mind is in constant turmoil. They have to look over their shoulders constantly as everything about their present life is a reminder of the war they left behind but which can easily catch up with them. Further reflections on the effects of the trauma associated with a constant reminder of war are seen in the poem *Home* where the refugee subject feels a shadow of their former self.

> Landed on new soil as a thick accented apparition you are like a ghost, shadow of former self. Ravages of war and the long journey from your former home take its toll on you.

The refugees face many struggles as they flee lost homes in search of new homes. This is in addition to the difficult decisions they must make in order to survive the journey. Sacrificing one's sense of dignity just to stay alive. Crossing into the host country is not a walk in the park. The eighth stanza opens with the words:

> no one would choose to crawl under fences, be beaten until your shadow leave you, raped, then drowned, forced to the bottom of the boat because you are darker, be sold, starved, shot at the border like a sick animal.

The refugee in order to save their life is reduced to behaviour that would normally be observed in hunted animals. The most vulnerable of the vulnerable, women and children risk being victims of rape, violence and exploitation, racial discrimination and loss of identity. To add to this, the grim reality that for most the camps will remain home to them for long periods of time, with no hope of getting asylum or assimilation into host countries and communities. The seventh line of the eighth stanza confirms this 'make a refugee camp a home for a year or two or ten'.

Conclusion

I observe that the author adopts a detached and impersonal voice and form which points to the reality of the situation.Through Shire's poetry we see the enduring human spirit shine through in the face of adversity. There is a hope and stubbornness in refugee poetry which forces the reader to make a critical assessment of the refugee crisis affecting the world.

Works cited

Achebe, Chinua. *Hopes and Impediments: selected essays*. London: Heinemann International, 1988.

Bell, Duncan (Ed). *Memory, Trauma and World Politics: Reflections on the Relationship between Past and Present*. New York: Palgrave Macmillan. 2006.

Said, Edward. *Reflections on Exile: and other literary and cultural essays*. Granta. 2012.

Shire, Warsan. *Our Men Do Not Belong to Us*. New York, Slapering Hol Press. 2014.

Teaching My Mother How To Give Birth.United Kingdom: Flipped Eye Publishing. 2011.

Internet sources

Hujale, Moulid. *A Refugee's Story*. http://www.irinnews.org/report/93527/kenya-somalia-refugees-story

Marta Bausells and Maeve Shearlaw. http://www.theguardian.com/book/2015/sep/16/poets-speak-out-for-refugees

15.

The wedding

Ciarunji Chesaina

This paper is a chapter from my novel in progress entitled *Diazipporah*. The idea of writing the novel was conceived when I lived for three years working in the Diaspora. This title is derived from the name of a major character in the novel called Zipporah. She has acquired the nickname 'Diazipporah' from her Kenyan compatriots who see her as an embodiment of Kenyan beauty in the Diaspora.

The action in the novel takes place everywhere in the Diaspora where Kenyans have emigrated to, although London seems to be a favourite city for the characters. Their attitude when they are leaving Kenya is that once they arrive in London, all their economic, political and social problems will be sorted out; only to be hit with a disheartening reality right at Heathrow Airport.

The novel revolves around the characters' struggles to survive in challenging and often hostile environments. Racial discrimination is assumed to have died a natural death with the passing of the twentieth century. Yet it seems to have taken more subtle and oppressive turns with the insecurity that is felt all over the globe. The initial discrimination with which Kenyans come face to face at the port of entry into the Diaspora is manifested through harassment in search of guns and explosives. Every black face is deemed guilty of terrorism until proven innocent. And the proof of innocence rests with the authorities in the foreign country.

The airports of the Diaspora present challenges. At other times one of the most challenging periods is when characters receive information from home demanding emergency travel home to attend to various issues. These might be serious sickness or death of loved ones. More often than not, a character is caught unawares when immigration papers are not in order. With luck, some characters have been able to fool immigration officers who think all black faces are the same. But some who are not so lucky have found themselves returned to

Kenya at the port of reentry into the Diaspora while their families are waiting to welcome them back.

Many Kenyans have high hopes about employment when they are leaving the country. Some assume, for instance that with education degrees of one field or another, the sky is the limit, only to be hit with unemployment and discrimination that they had not anticipated when they left Kenya. Employers out there wish to employ Kenyans because they are known to be honest and hardworking. However, this is mainly in manual work, whether one is educated or not. Even after accepting a blue collar job, a Kenyan experiences discrimination with regard to remuneration as well as other terms of employment.

People who fled political, economic as well as social issues in Kenya are the worst hit by difficult struggles to survive in the Diaspora. On the one hand, they would like to socialize with fellow Kenyans in order to feel at home away from home. On the other hand, they are perpetually plagued with the fear of coming face to face with a compatriot who knows about their histories at home.

Cultural conflict is an important theme in the novel *Diazipporah*. This is not merely on the level of Western versus Kenyan cultures. It also extends in diverse ways to conflict between cultures of various Kenyan communities represented in the Diaspora. It is true that there are general networks of fellow Kenyans out there. However, in some areas Kenyans in the Diaspora form stronger ties with those from their own ethnic backgrounds.

Intermarriage across ethnic groups is encouraged but various cultural and social conflicts are experienced. There are tendencies to exaggerate certain cultural practices from back home, for instance with regard to dowry. Commercialization of dowry is exaggerated in the Diaspora due to pressure from expectations of parents back home. It is assumed that young men living in the Diaspora are loaded with money. Hence when any of them wishes to marry they are confronted with hefty demands from future in-laws. The chapter 'The Wedding', therefore, tackles some of the cultural conflicts experienced by Kenyans in the Diaspora. It will be observed that the struggle to be accepted as a *bona fide* member of the Kenyan community in the Diaspora is most Kenyans' aspiration!

The Wedding

Elizabeth had been baking the whole week. She had to request to be allocated night duty this week. That way she was able to bake and organize her sitting room during the day. And of course she was able to squeeze in a quick wink. She did not want to doze off during the night duty. Oh! No! That would be a disaster.

It was not easy working as a nurse in a big and busy hospital like the Queen

Victoria. But Elizabeth loved her work. She loved her patients….In fact she loved everyone. She loved her colleagues; seniors, equals and even juniors. Everyone and everybody who came across Elizabeth just fell in love with her. That was how the most reserved doctor at the hospital had fallen in love with her. And this happened at the most weird of places within the hospital – the operating theatre.

It was not her looks; for he did not see her face. It was not her shape, for he could not see her physique. How could he when she was dressed in theatre garb. It was nothing physical. It was just the aura around her as she handled her duty during that operation. It was the ambiance she created in the theatre. So a few days later, the doctor called her into his office. He did not know how to begin, this was not something he did every day; inviting a lady out? Where would he take her? Would she agree, anyway? Where could he find the time? He was a busy doctor, working in the busiest of hospitals. And his first duty was to his patients. What if the lady refused his invitation? He had only to try.

'Sister Elizabeth,' Dr Ratfield always used the full name of any of the nurses. 'Yes, doctor,' answered Sister Liz, as her colleagues called her.

'I was just wondering…'

Sister Liz too was wondering. As she stood there in his office, she noticed that his hand was shaking. She wondered whether the problem was the case the doctor was writing about. She had worked under him in various cases, but she had never seen him so perturbed. The operation he had performed recently, though somewhat complicated, had been successful. What was troubling Dr Ratfied this afternoon?

'Yes doctor,' Sister Liz responded.

'I was just wondering,' Dr Ratfield repeated. 'Yes doctor.'

'If you would like to have some ice cream.' 'Ice cream in winter?' asked sister Liz surprised. 'Nice winter ice cream,' the doctor assured her. 'Oh! Yes of course,' sister Liz quickly said to put the doctor at ease. She had never heard of such a thing as winter ice cream, but then she had never been invited by a doctor for ice cream.

'Nice winter ice cream would be nice, doctor', she added.

'What do you say we go for ice cream this evening, say eight o'clock?' asked Dr Ratfield. 'I have a patient to see at seven, but his is just a review.'

'Oh! I'm sorry, doctor, tonight I'm going out for coffee with the girls, some of my fellow nurses.'

'Going out for coffee, Sister Elizabeth?'

'Yes doctor, with the girls.'

Dr Ratfield pondered for a minute. The sweat on his brow was becoming unbearable. So he took some tissue and did a bit of wiping. Elizabeth noticed this and wished she had not mentioned the Nurses' Coffee Evening.

'I could offer you coffee as well,' Dr Ratfield said, with greater confidence this time.

'Oh! Yes, doctor… I love coffee with my winter ice cream,' she quickly said.

'That's settled then, coffee and ice cream at eight tonight.'

They went to a pleasant café far from the Queen Victoria Hospital. Whether the doctor was avoiding an accidental meeting with the girls' coffee crew, Elizabeth was not sure. They had coffee with warm muffins and English tea cakes. In order not to disappoint the doctor, Elizabeth ordered ice cream. She thought she saw the doctor smile at the corner of his lips, but she was going to have the 'winter ice cream,' anyway.

The doctor did not talk much but Elizabeth noticed he kept stealing glances at her face. Immediately she was dropped at her place, she called her mum.

'Are you awake, mum?' she started.

'Oh! Yes, how are you?'

'Fine,' she said, 'but a little disturbed'.

'What happened, honey?' asked the mum, a bit worried.

'Oh! Nothing much, really… I just had this weird date… well… I don't think I can call it that really.'

'A date my honey? Who was it? I'm all ears!' the mum was most excited.

'Mum, don't get all worked up… it was this … this… this doctor I've worked under many times…'

'Go for it, dear. I've been telling you…'

'It's not what you think… I just wanted to tell you… The funny thing about it, he invited me for ice cream and coffee, what a weird thing…' 'Well, your father was worse. He took me to the park in winter. He had carried two small packets of popcorn… and he proposed to me with his mouth full of popcorn.'

'This is nothing like a proposal, mum. But you know what? He did not talk much, but I kinda like him.'

'You must bring him round…'

'Mum, I've got to go. I'll talk to you tomorrow. Bye.'

'Bye, dear.'

A month later, Dr Ratfield invited Sister Liz to an expensive restaurant for a dinner this time. Elizabeth enjoyed the food and the doctor's company. It was her turn to sweat. It was her fingers' turn to shake, for the doctor did not waste any time. After the desert, he waited for Elizabeth to finish her coffee. While she waited for her ice cream which seemed to take forever, Dr George Ratfield proposed to her and put an engagement ring on her finger. That difficult part done and dusted, they were married a year later.

♦

That was almost thirty years ago. Now she had her pastries and other goodies to prepare. Elizabeth loved baking. She loved trying different pastries. She had recently learnt how to make samosas, and she was happy that her husband loved taking a few to his office for his tea break. Her son was not keen, but then today he would appreciate them to tickle the taste buds of his many friends. More than the taste buds, the friends would need to be kept in good humour in order to be of good behaviour in an alcohol-free function. This was one of the functions in which no alcohol was served at Dr Ratfield's residence.

It was a special function.

The son's fiancée and her family (actually more the family) were coming to officially see the home of the bridegroom-to-be. The doctor's Kikuyu friends had tried to explain to him the cultural meaning of the ceremony and he was delighted to learn that it was not yet another opportunity for more money to be paid before the wedding. Already, he had given the in-laws so much money that he wondered if the whole thing was not trickery.

It had started with a ceremony called, *kuhandaithigi* where so many charges had been levied. They had simply gone – Dr Ratfield's family and his friends – to visit the girl's home and officially state the young man's intention to wed the girl. Dr Ratfield was not mean in spending his money, but then any intelligent person wanted to understand the various expenses. The first shock was when they were given the bills of the groceries and drinks at the ceremony to settle. Surely they were the visitors and visitors are never asked to pay for what they had eaten in the home. The doctor's Kikuyu friends had taken the bills to cool the temperatures before the other shocking charges were brought forward.

The dowry was more than a shocker. The girl's aunt produced a huge figure of the money she claimed to have spent educating the girls. This did not include the ridiculous amount claimed to cover for all the utensils the girl was said to have broken in the home since arriving from Kenya. The bridegroom-to-be had been charged some unfathomable amount for 'disrespect and insubordination'. It was explained to him that he should not have shaken hands with the aunts and the uncles of the girl. Yet it was these in-laws, who had readily extended their hands. But then the doctor's Kikuyu friends had warned his son not to show any sign of annoyance. This could lead to complete refusal to release the girl for marriage.

A little drama at the end of the *kuhandaithigi* served as the icing on the cake. All along, as the goings on were unfolding, the girl was absent. When everything had been settled and huge holes had been pierced into Dr Ratfields' pockets, his escorts said they wanted to greet the bride-to-be.

'Which girl?' an aunt asked wearing a very serious face?

Shock on the faces of Dr Ratfield's team's face. '*uuu! Ukai na guku.* Come, come all of you.'

At this point other aunts came from all directions bearing weapons of cooking sticks, ladles and even kitchen knives. Now the doctor's people were more shocked. But the real shocker was yet to come.

'You must have wandered into the wrong homestead,' another aunt said.

'Young man,' a third aunt challenged the doctor's son. 'Did you lie to your people that you had seen a girl in this homestead?'

The best-man-to-be moved forward. He was a better actor than these aunts.

'Our mothers,' he said in a plaintive voice. 'We only wandered into this homestead to find out if a girl of our age lives here. We did not mean any harm. Forgive wayward children.'

'All right,' said the challenger. 'Wait there.' All the escorts of the doctor's son surrounded him, forming a canopy around him. They did not know what to expect, but they were not leaving before seeing the girl.

As if on cue, a group of veiled women arrived on the scene. Each was covered completely with *khangas* of all colours. The doctor's son was not prepared for this but the best- man-to-be seemed prepared for it. So he whispered something to his friend. Then the challenger moved forward.

'These are all the girls in this homestead which one did you ever see in your life?'

The young men started moving forward.

'No! No! No!' The challenger shouted.

'Not all of you!'

'Aah! Aah! Aah!' responded the young men.

Ignoring them, the challenger pointed at the doctor's son and told him to move close to her.

'I want you to walk around and show me the girl you imagined lived in this homestead,' she told him. 'And don't touch' she added.

'Ooh! Ooh! Ooh!' the escorts said in unison. The challenger ignored them.

The doctor's son walked methodically from one woman (or set of *khangas*) to another. It was difficult to discover his beloved, with all these coverings. Then suddenly he stopped in front of one set of *khangas*. The girl's favourite perfume gave him the clue and without fearing the challenger, he uncovered her face and planted a big kiss on her lips. He was charged an exorbitant amount for the kiss, but this did not pain.

Elizabeth was happy that *itara* was the last ceremony before the wedding. She did not mind entertaining and at times she actually enjoyed it. However, it was not easy entertaining Kenyans. It could be exhausting. First, you could not estimate the number of guests to cater for. Kenyans in Diazipporah believed that a party was an occasion for them to be at home away from home; especially if that party happened to be at Daktari's. And many a time people made it happen to be at Daktari's and why not? Daktari was not only their friend but their doctor as well. His wife was their mother, nurse and counsellor, all rolled into one. Their only child was getting married. This called for a big and long period of celebrations.

Every time their son's fiancée visited, Dr Ratfield and Elizabeth loved her better than the previous time she had become like a daughter to them. At times, their son suspected that her arrival in his life filled the gap created by the lack of a daughter in the family. She was the daughter the doctor and Elizabeth never had. She was a very well behaved child and she never showed characteristic of children orphaned at an early age. Her aunt had done an excellent job of filling the gap left by her mother and father when they died in a road accident in Kenya.

♦

They could not have chosen a better season for the wedding. It was summer; warm summer. The birds were singing joyfully and in this part of the country, there were various types of birds. Small birds, medium sized birds, big birds. The small birds were the best. They were beautiful, colourful and had melodious voices. They sang, they danced, they talked. The birds' dancing and singing synchronized with that of the humans. Love was indeed in the air.

The woman had arrived from Kenya that morning and she was glad the weather was so good. It was warm and pleasant. Joy was in the air, but this was the complete opposite of what she was feeling inside. There was turbulence there. She was jetlagged, but that was not it. She had freshened up and changed her clothes. That had done wonders on her body, but still the turbulence remained.

When an African person and a white person come together and make a baby, something out of this world happens. It is not the physique and it is not the psyche. It is not a mistake and it is not what you are thinking. It is something unique. A creature full of beauty and grace comes out. Young Dr Ratteng was such a creature. Old Dr George Ratfield and Nurse Elizabeth must have been well prepared when they made their baby.

He was now six foot four, a whole three inches taller than his father.

'You are driving too slowly,' said the woman. 'You will make me late.'

'I am trying my best,' replied the taximan.

'Not your very best,' said the woman with irritation. 'Why have you stopped now?'

'The lights are red,' said the taximan calmly. 'Surely you can go!' shouted the woman. 'There is no policeman in sight.'

The taximan just laughed. He was from Nigeria and the story of jumping lights was just too familiar. In Africa but not here.

The church was packed. It was splitting at the seams. Every Kenyan was here. They outnumbered Elizabeth's relations by far. Which Kenyan could miss Daktari's son's wedding. Even people who never stepped in a church were here. Like Solo and Kevin. Solomon's nickname was 'Mankind', and it was more popular than 'Solo'. He had very limited English vocabulary. So when he was asked why he was a self-styled bodyguard for Kevin he had responded.

'Because is also a Mankind…. He is not a monkey.'

If there were two people Mankind could die for, it was Dr Ratfield and Kevin. Dr Ratfield had rehabilitated Solomon when he had one foot in the grave. He almost died from the effects of alcohol and drug abuse. That was why he was so devoted to the doctor. And as for being Kevin's bodyguard, Solomon believed that if the Daktari had managed to save him from death, he could easily save Kevin. The latter was worse than Solomon was, but Solo thought otherwise. He had made it his business to escort Kevin to all parties, just to keep an eye. This morning they had sat at the back of the church, just in case.

The bride was taking too long to arrive at the church. One of the grooms telephoned to say they had encountered a small problem but they were sorting it out. Apparently, when they arrived at the aunt's place the key to the gate got lost. While they were wondering if to assist breaking the gate, one of the women on the groom's inside said that was not necessary. She asked the grooms to put some money together and they were puzzled. Everything else was like a little drama. The woman and her colleagues started dancing and singing songs whose words the grooms could not decipher. As soon as the money was pushed under the gap to the other side, the gate key was found and out came the girl and her aunt.

They arrived at the church entrance just as 'Amazing Grace' was ending. The pianist immediately started on 'Here Comes the Bride', and everyone was up on their feet. Their heads were turned in the direction of the new arrivals and everyone wanted to catch a glimpse of the bride. Fortunately, she was not wearing one of those white gowns which include a veil mask for the face. She wore beautiful, purple African attire made of real *kente* cloth from Ghana.

Her name was Diazipporah. It was a nickname but she had officially adopted it. Her real name in Kenya was Zipporah, but on her arrived here fellow Kenyan students said 'Zipporah' was too commonplace to describe such a beautiful girl. After all, she was deemed to be an epitome of Kenyan beauty in the Diaspora and so what would be a more fitting name than Diazipporah? She was a tall girl, very tall. Her hair was long and she always insisted on braiding it down the back in African *coiffure* of corn rows. Her smooth face was dark, the colour of those Kenyan beans called *njahi;* these were the beans used in Kenya to feed newly delivered women. The beans were said to be very rich in proteins. If Diazipporah had been a Kalenjin, her name would have been, Kaptuiya, black beauty. When she smiled, her upper four teeth revealed a gap in the middle; a gap considered a sign of beauty among many communities in Kenya.

As the congregation watched young Dr Ratteng and Diazipporah, they could feel the deep love between them. They were opposite in looks for one was very light while the other was very dark. However, they looked like peas in a pod in their features especially on the lips. It was true what people in Kenya always said; that people always sought as marriage partners those who resembled them. But other people said, living together made couples resemble each other.

The pastor did not want to waste any more time. He now signaled the pianist to bring the music to a stop. After the second reading, he went straight into calling the parents of the bride to move forward, ready to give her away. The aunt had marshalled (or paid) an uncle of some sort to stand in for the deceased father.

'Now the moment has come to join the youngest couple in Diazipporah. Yet the church requires we give a chance to anyone who might have a valid reason why these two should not be married.'

Now, turning to the couple he asked; 'Joseph and Diazipporah, is there any reason why you should not be joined together in holy matrimony?'

Peals of laughter from the congregation.

'I must ask them first,' said the pastor in a serious tone.

'No,' the couple said in unison.

Now he looked straight at the congregation and asked.

'Is there anybody who has any valid reason why

these two should not be joined together in holy matrimony?'

Of course there was none and everyone was here to witness the beginning of a happy marriage.

'If there is anyone,' the pastor continued. 'Speak now or forever hold your peace.'

The pastor now started the business of the day. He asked for wedding rings to be brought close to him. He first gave young Dr Ratteng the ring for the bride.

'Repeat after me...I, Joseph Ratteng... 'Wait...wait...wait,' a woman rushed in panting. 'Pastor wait!'

She went straight to the front and stood between young Dr Ratteng and Diazipporah. Then in a plaintive but loud voice she said:

'Pastor, they cannot be married. The two are brother and sister...'

Then she left as suddenly as she had come and went straight to her waiting taxi. The silence that fell in the church could be cut with a knife. Kevin was the first to recover.

'But of course the reception will go on...'

'Shut up Kevo,' said Solo escorting Kevin outside. One by one, the congregation left, starting with the people at the back.

About the contributors

Ciarunji Chesaina is a Professor of Literature at University of Nairobi. She holds PhD and MA degrees in Literature from University of Leeds in the UK; a Master of Education from Harvard University (USA) and a Master of Business Administration from USIU (Africa). In the course of her career, Prof. Chesaina has held various positions of leadership. At University of Nairobi she has served as Director of International Programmes of the University as well as representative of College of Humanities to the Board of Postgraduate Studies. Professor Chesaina served as Kenya's Ambassador to the Republic of South Africa in the years 2000 to 2003. She has published widely in her area of specialization in Literature as well as in other fields. She is the author of 'Pokot'; 'Oral Literature of the Kalenjin'; 'Oral Literature of Embu and Mbeere' and 'Hope in the Horizon' among other texts. She has written many national papers and made presentations and was one of the three scholars who drafted Kenya's position paper on 'Environmental Education' presented at Tbilisi in 1979. In 1993, she was one of Kenya's representatives at the World Conference in Costa Rica where she presented a paper on 'Women's Education in Kenya'. Currently she is engaged in writing creative works. She has already published several short stories and is about to complete her first novel.

Yash Pal Ghai: Prof. Yash Pal Ghai, born in Ruiru, Kenya, retired as professor of law from the University of Hong Kong in 2013 after 40 years of law teaching. He helped to set up the first law school, in Dar es Salaam, which served five African countries, and became the first East African Law Dean. He has taught at several leading universities in the USA, Europe and Asia. His principal area of research has been public law, in a broad and comparative form. He has published over 20 books, some as editor and contributor, and nearly 200 articles. His other main pursuit has been constitution making. In addition to his contribution to the 2010 Kenya constitution, he assisted in several other countries, including Somalia in 2011, Seychelles, Tanganyika, Maldives, Nepal, Papua New Guinea, Solomon Islands, Vanuatu, Fiji, Iraq and Afghanistan. He was adviser to the Dalai Lama in his government's negotiations with China on Tibetan autonomy, and acted as a mediator between the Nagas and the Indian Government. For a long time he has participated in civil society organisations. He established a non-racial NGO in Fiji which is today its leading NGO. In Kenya, he has started the Katiba Institute together with Jill Cottrell and Waikwa Wanyoike.

James Orao has taught Intercultural German Studies at the Department of

Linguistics and Languages at the University of Nairobi since 2005. He holds an MA degree in Intercultural German Studies from University of Nairobi and a PhD in German Studies from University of Münster in Germany. In 2014 he published his book *Selbstverortungen – Migration und Identität in der zeitgenössischen deutsch- und englischsprachigen Migrationsliteratur* (Peter Lang) (Intercultural Narrations – Migrations and Identities in the contemporary German- and English-speaking Immigrants' Literature). His areas of research interest include Comparative Literature, Inter- and Transcultural Literature and Contemporary Literatures in English and German. His other publications include: *Metaphern der Migration: die Figurationen des Reisens in der zeitgenössischen deutschsprachigen Migrationsliteratur* (2014) and *Migrationsliteratur und die Großstadtliteratur: Neue Zugänge zu einem alten Thema* (2011). Dr Orao has also taught German Studies at Kenyatta University in Nairobi and Moi University in Eldoret.

Judith Jai Jefwa is presently a lecturer in the Department of Literature at University of Nairobi where she began teaching in 2000. She is a trained teacher of English and Literature and obtained both her undergraduate and Masters' degrees in literature from Kenyatta University in Nairobi. She also holds a PhD degree in Literature from University of Nairobi. Before joining University of Nairobi she taught in various high schools in Kenya where she developed her skills in play writing and production as well as creative writing. Subsequently she did a lot of play writing and production and adjudication of plays at the Kenya Schools' and Colleges' Drama festivals held annually in Kenya. In the area of creative writing, she has published two children's story books, *Matilda na Salama* and *Daudi Kiwete*. The books have been on the Kenyan primary schools' reading list for many years. Her teaching areas at University of Nairobi have been European and African Drama. However, her current research interests include studies in literature and culture and children's literature. She has a special interest in developing reading materials for children in English, Kiswahili and Lulogoli, a local language in Kenya. She is also interested in how literature presents the manner in which cultural practices affect people especially in areas of health, palliative care and end of life issues. Her interest is in seeing the meeting point between literature, culture and real life experiences.

Joseph Muleka is a writer, critic, scholar, musician and educationist. He holds a PhD in Literature from University of Nairobi and is currently a senior lecturer in the Department of Literature, University of Nairobi. He has published in numerous local and international journals, on subjects of literature, culture, theory and gender. His complete works in the latter area include *Images of Women in African Oral Literature* and *Girl Characters in Children's Books: A Patriarchal Portrait*. He has also written student guides, short stories and story books for junior readers. Some of the titles for the junior readers' category include: *Naomi and the Cannibals*; *Naomi in her New School*; *Naomi the*

Detective (Nominated for The Wahome Mutahi Prize for Literature, 2014); *Naomi's Stories*; *Naomi and Cindy* and *Lion the King*. He is now in the process of collecting poetry under the title 'Three Sides of a Coin' and editing an anthology of short stories by the title *The Brick Fence*. Muleka also holds a Certificate in Teacher Education – P1 from Mosoriot College; Dip. Ed (Kagumo College); B.Ed (The Catholic University of Eastern Africa) and MA in Literature (Kenyatta University). Joseph studied at Mundika School and St Paul's Amukura, before joining Mosoriot College for a certificate course in teaching. He later joined Kagumo College to study Music and Kiswahili. He then studied at Catholic University of Eastern Africa for his Bachelor of Education specializing in English and Literature. After teaching in several schools, he joined Kenyatta University for his MA in Literature and University of Nairobi for his Ph.D. His recent publication: *Images of Women in African Oral Literature* is a research carried out in Kenya. He has authored *Introduction to Prose*, currently used by students of literature as well as written study guides and contributed to various academic publications and journals.

Wandia Njoya is based at Daystar University in Kenya, where she is the head of the Department of Language and Performing Arts.

Sarah Nkuchia-Kyalo is an afro-optimist who has worked for over six years on human rights and social justice work in East Africa. Trained in social sciences and international relations; her academic and professional interests focus on economic justice, critical philanthropy and Pan-Africanism. She currently works at the Open Society Initiative for Eastern Africa on economic justice.

Lencer Achieng' Ndede is a Lecturer at Kabarak University. She holds a B.Ed from Moi University and an MA in Literature from University of Nairobi; and is currently a PhD Student in Literature at University of Nairobi. She is an Adjudicator in Music and Drama and is very passionate about development of Literature and has written and presented a number papers at various Literature, Drama, Film and Music conferences.

Tom Odhiambo is a senior lecturer at University of Nairobi. He teaches undergraduate and postgraduate courses in literature; is a researcher and coordinator of the B.Ed program in Arts and Literature. He also supervises MA and PhD research candidates in the Department of Literature and MA candidates in the School of Journalism and Mass Communication.

Jairus Omuteche teaches literature in the Department of Language and Literature Education at Masinde Muliro University of Science and Technology in Kakamega, Kenya. He holds an MA in Literature from University of Nairobi and a PhD in Comparative Literature from University of Sunderland, UK. His research and teaching interests focus on comparative World Literature; postcolonial theory; theorising Globalisation, Immigration, Cosmopolitanism, and Diaspora; Life Writing; African Oral Literature; and how they relate to issues of Home, Identity, and Belonging. He has done studies and published critical essays in refereed journals and as book chapters on the works of Yusuf Dawood, M G Vassanji, Chika Unigwe, Toni Morrison, Alice Walker, Assata Shakur, Dionne Brand, Edwidge Danticat among other writers who grapple with the themes of diasporicity, migration and globalisation. Among his recent publications are his edited book of critical essays, *Critical Readings on East African Autobiography* (Gelda Verlag Publishers, *2016)*; 'Resisting Exclusion in African American Writing', published in *Journal of African Literature and Culture, No. 12*, 2015; and 'Case Study: Teaching two Caribbean Texts in Kenyan University' published in *Ariel* Vol. 46, January-April, 2015.

Simon Peter Otieno is a graduate of Catholic University of Eastern Africa (B.Ed), University of Nairobi (M.A Literature) and University of Leeds (Ph.D). He is a writer, director and critic of theatre and film; and a coordinator of film production in schools, colleges and universities for the Ministry of Education in Kenya. He is currently teaching theatre and film studies at University of Nairobi.

Jane Nambiri Ouma is a Research Fellow at the Directorate of Research, Innovation and Graduate Training at Catholic University of Eastern Africa (CUEA), where she collaborates the research activities for the university. She holds a B.Ed in History and Christian Religious Education and an MA in Educational Research and Evaluation from CUEA, Kenya. She has offered research consultancy services to various multi-donor organization projects both as a researcher and analyst including 'Stop Violence against Girls' in a school project funded by Lottery Fund through Action Aid International Kenya, National Cohesion and Integration Commission (NCIC)-Kenya and Centre for Policy Research-Kenya. Her recent publications include: 'Fifty Years of Boy Child Education in Kenya: A Paradigm Shift'; 'Homogenizing Continental Africa and its Diaspora through lessons on African Oral Social Culture' and 'the Influence of Angela Merici's Spirituality: A Postmodern Challenge in Kenya'. Jane Ouma's research interests are in the areas of African spirituality, gender issues, evaluation and education.

Lynda Ouma is a Literature student studying for an MA at University of Nairobi. Her ambition is to utilize the skills and knowledge she has acquired so far to develop into a professional media and communication expert whose aim is to write and produce stories that leave a positive impact on the community. She has expertise in Script writing for TV and Radio news broadcasts, Feature Writing, Social Media Skills, Audio Editing, Literature review and analysis as well as Voice Over reading. Some of her works include literary contributions to the high school set book *Whale Rider* by Witi Ihimaera for the Kenya Institute of Education; as well as three articles which were published in a young writers' anthology titled *Away with words across the miles* edited by Heather

Killingray. Lynda spends some time each month volunteering in her community by teaching.

John Sibi-Okumu is a Kenyan broadcaster and actor-director-playwright, based in Nairobi. He has played many lead roles on-stage, including Romeo, Lysander, Shylock, Oberon, Oedipus, Krapp and Vladimir. He features on-screen in *The Constant Gardener; Shake Hands with The Devil!; The First Grader* and *The Rugged Priest,* among other films. Under his direction, Kenyan musician Eric Wainaina's *Mo Faya!* was received with great acclaim in the USA at the New York Festival of Musical Theatre 2009, before enjoying a record breaking, homecoming reception at The Godown Arts' Centre in Nairobi. He has authored six original plays: *Role Play – a Journey into the Kenyan Psyche; Minister, karibu!; Meetings; Dinner with Her Excellency; Elements* and *Kaggia* and also devised *In Search of the Drum Major* and *Like Ripples on a Pond* (both on the American Civil Rights Movement) as well as *Milestones – a Showcase for African Poetry.*

Kanyi Thiong'o holds a B.Ed in English and Literature, and an MA in Literature. He is currently a PhD candidate in University of Nairobi's Department of Literature and teaches Literature at Egerton University. His major research focuses on literary meanings derived from sound engineering techniques in Music, Film, Theatre and Performing Arts. At present, he is working on an Audio Poetic theory, which can be employed to study literary meanings in songs and oral performances. In addition, he has carried out research on Cultural Myths of the Luo in Luo Nyanza and Sumba Districts; Oral Poetry of the Digo and the Duruma in Mombasa; The Place of Literature in Gikuyu Popular Music in Nairobi and The role of Urban Popular songs in the development of Urban Identities. He has been teaching Literature in various Universities for the last seven years where he has specialized in: Theory and Criticism; Creative writing in Fiction and Drama; Poetry; Critical Reading and Response; Stylistics; Folklore and Oral Literature studies, Theories and Methods in Oral Literature; East African Drama and Poetry; Language Description and Use; East African Prose; Critical Writing; Critical Reading and African Drama. In addition, he is a board member of Kenya Oral Literature Association (KOLA). He has authored several creative works of Art, prose fiction and several collections of poetry and a self-help book titled *Becoming what you Want.* Outside academics, he teaches song writing, vocal training, directing performances and music production.

About the editors

Zahid Rajan is a graphic designer by profession. He has combined these skills with social activism and publishing in the realms of justice, human rights and democracy. He is the executive editor of *AwaaZ* magazine, director of the SAMOSA Festival, chair of the Kenya Palestine Solidarity Movement and an active participant in Kenya's civil rights movement.

Zarina Patel is a physiotherapist turned author who has studied South Asian history in Kenya and written several books on its nationalist leaders and journalists. She is the granddaughter of the Kenyan pioneer, Alibhai Mulla Jeevanjee, and single-handedly 'saved' Jeevanjee Gardens in Nairobi from land grabbers. She is the Managing Editor of *AwaaZ* magazine, co-founder of the SAMOSA Festival and a human rights activist and environmentalist.

Acknowledgements

The organizing team (comprised of Anna Mwangi Prof Muleka, Dr Makau Kitata, Zahid Rajan and Zarina Patel) and the SAMOSA team would like to thank the Literature Department of the University of Nairobi and its Chair, Dr Masumi Odari, for organizing the Colloquium on 'Citizenship, Identity and Belonging' and hosting the joint event. Our thanks to the contributors for being able to submit papers at rather short notice, but which ensured interesting and lively discussions at the colloquium. Our thanks to Prof Peter Wasamba, Dean Faculty of Arts, for opening the event, and to the discussants, Prof H Indangasi, Prof M Mweseli, Prof H Mwanzi, Prof Alina Rikanya, Dr G Siundu, and Prof Chris Wanjala for their lively inputs.

The SAMOSA 2016 team was led by Zahid Rajan, the Festival Director. The members of the team were: Deputy Festival Director, Ubax Abdi; Stefania Tranfo; John Namai; Narissa Alibhai; Reema Doshi; Sadia Ahmed and Zarina Patel. We wish to thank all our partners and supporters who helped to make SAMOSA 2016 such a success.

Our thanks also for the support of the following:

Corporates

Basco Paints, Concorde Car Hire & Safaris, Dura Coat, Eastleigh Mall Ltd, Giro Commercial Bank Ltd, I&M Bank, St Austin's Service Station Ltd, Sunny River, Uber, Bites

Event Partners

Fatumas Voice, The GoDown, Kilimanjaro Restaurant, Jesuit Refugee Services, Kenya Dialogues Project, Kenya Human Rights Commission, PAWA 254, Roffeke, Society for International Development, University of Nairobi Department of Literature, YogaKenya.org, Zamaleo ACT

Media Partners

Asian Weekly, Bloom Agency, EastFM, InformAction, KenyaBuzz, StarFM, The Star

Philanthropic Organisations

The Chandaria Foundation, Victoria Commercial Bank

Venue Partners

Alliance Française, Nairobi, The Kenyan Cultural Centre, Palace Hotel, Pawa254, Sarakasi

Twinning Partner

Tradizionandu